KETO VEGAN

Cookbook For Beginners

Healthy, Easy & Affordable VEGAN Recipes to Weight Lose with 28 -Days Meal Plans

BY

Rowe R. Leon

Keto Vegan Cookbook For Beginners

Table of Content

INTRODUCTION

Can one even follow a vegan-keto diet? These two diets appear to be diametrically opposed at first. The ketogenic diet calls for high fat and low carbs from animal sources, while vegan diets call for high carbs and low fat from plant sources. However, the two can be combined in a magical way to create a diet that ensures fat loss, lowered cholesterol, increased energy, and superior brain health.

No matter your motivation for going vegan, you are not restricted from following the ketogenic diet, which is a high-fat eating plan. You will learn everything you need to know in this book about putting together a diet that will nourish your body and support your metabolism. Additionally, it will give you advice on how to incorporate exercise, consume adequate nutrients, handle unfavorable situations, and prevent the keto flu.

Finally, there are many recipes that can help you spice up your diet so that you are more likely to stick to it. There are also some suggestions for vegan-keto cooking. Our seven-day meal plan will make it easier for you to get used to this diet and stick with it.

You will be an authority on the vegan-keto diet by the time this book is finished. You'll be prepared to begin this remarkable diet and reap all of its health advantages.

The Vegan-Keto Diet

The vegan keto diet is a welcome one! The vegan keto diet offers an alternative to the typical animal fats and proteins found in the ketogenic diet for those looking to shed some lbs and improve their health. Let's go over how the ketogenic diet and veganism operate so that you can comprehend how to combine these two diets to create a potently wholesome and slimming combination.

What is the Vegan Diet?

Animal products of any kind should not be included in a healthy vegan diet. Vegans typically adhere to this diet because they are concerned about the daily environmental and animal rights abuses that are committed by the meat industry. The vegan diet is not only ethical, though. It also has significant advantages for bettering blood glucose regulation. [1] The majority of vegan consumers also mention significant weight loss. [1] According to studies, vegans typically have lower BMIs than non-vegans. [1]

It's not always as simple as avoiding animal products when following a vegan diet. In fact, it takes a fair amount of math to figure out how to stay away from animal products while still getting enough nutrition. Several variations of veganism exist:

- **The whole-food vegan diet:** Only unprocessed whole foods, such as fruits, vegetables, whole grains, legumes, nuts, and seeds, are allowed on this diet.
- **The raw-food vegan diet:** Whole foods must be uncooked or cooked to a temperature below 118°F (48°C) in this diet. This

diet calls for raw food without plants that are high in fat, like nuts or avocados. Instead, consumers are advised to munch on raw fruits and vegetables. This eating plan is also referred to as a fruitarian diet or a low-fat, raw-food vegan diet.

- **The Starch Solution:** This diet differs from the low-fat, raw-food vegan one in that it calls for a lot of high-carbohydrate foods rather than fruit, such as potatoes or rice. These two variations are very similar in every other way.
- **Raw till 4:** Here, one consumes raw foods up until four and then cooked plants.
- **The junk-food vegan diet:** Some vegans rely on vegan "junk" foods that have undergone extensive processing, like cheese or snacks.

The vegan-keto diet differs from other vegan diets in that it places a greater emphasis on consuming high levels of protein and fat than it does on carbohydrates. Actually, on this diet you shouldn't be consuming any carbs at all. Contrary to popular belief, consuming junk food—even vegan junk food—is not necessary to obtain these nutrients. Whole, raw foods like avocados, nuts, and coconuts as well as dietary supplements like spirulina, wheat grass juice powder, coconut oils, and vegetable oils can provide you with a lot of fat and protein.

What is the Keto Diet?

The ketogenic diet, also known as the "keto diet," is a way of eating that makes your body burn fat quickly. You must abstain from all sugars and carbohydrates, and only consume protein and fat to fuel your body. By doing this, you'll put your body into ketosis, a metabolic state in which it uses fat for fuel because it doesn't have any sugar to burn. This diet can result in rapid and amazing weight loss.

Here is a quick explanation of how this diet functions while we go into greater detail about how to implement it properly in the following chapter:

You usually eat carbohydrates. In fact, more carbs are recommended in most diets than any other nutrient. Your body transforms that into glucose, which supplies energy to your cells. However, the ketogenic diet contains almost no carbohydrates. This forces your liver to start producing ketones and fatty acids from the fats it consumes. Now, instead of using glucose for energy, your body must run on ketone bodies. You should still eat 5% of your diet as carbohydrates even if you follow the keto diet because only 5% of your cells cannot use these as a source of fuel. 12 On this diet, your body starts using ketones as its primary energy source. This means that in addition to burning all of the fat in your body's reserves to help you lose weight through a process known as ketosis, your body will also use the fat in your diet as a source of energy.

You can only enter this state of ketosis by cutting carbs out of your diet almost entirely. As long as the amount of carbs and sugar is minimal, some carbs are acceptable, such as a few berries in the morning. An apple or a glass of milk contains about 10-35 grams of the daily recommended carbohydrate intake. Keep in mind that there are healthy carbohydrates that come from whole foods and unhealthy carbohydrates that originate from processed foods, wheat, or white grains like white rice. You should typically consume 80–90% of your daily calories as fat.

Animal products like bacon, hot dogs, and milk are the main sources of all of this fat for most people. Although the diet may not always permit more fruits and vegetables, some people do. True keto diet adheres very strictly to the carb deficit parameters, so eating lots of fruits and vegetables is not recommended.

Your body starts burning fat as a result of the diet. However, a recent study discovered that the weight loss is actually brought on by the carbohydrate restriction. By avoiding carbohydrates, you can lessen your cravings for them and eventually get over them. This indicates that as you stick with the diet longer, it becomes simpler to follow.

You can check your urine for ketones using a Ketostix or another ke tone-measuring device to see if you are in ketosis. Your body is not in ketosis if your blood ketones are not high enough.

Thus, it appears that vegetarians and vegans cannot follow the keto diet because it heavily relies on animal proteins and fats. The pillars of the keto diet are butter, cheese, and meat. However, the reality is that you can eat a vegan diet and still adhere to it, especially in this day and age when there have been so many advances in healthy food.

Challenges of the Keto Diet

There are two main difficulties with the keto diet that devotees encounter.

The first is the initial round of uncomfortable side effects that appear as your body rids itself of carbohydrates. This detox is frequently referred to as "the keto flu" and can be uncomfortable and strenuous. People don't start this diet expecting to feel sick to their stomachs, crampy, exhausted, or otherwise unwell. However, the keto flu is only a passing condition. The diet also has other drawbacks, like bad breath. Gum, good oral hygiene, and eating some fruit can all help with this.

Another difficulty is actual cravings for carbohydrates. Carb cravings will disappear for those following this diet, but it will take time. In fact, sugar and carbohydrates are very addictive. Your body starts to depend on them for satisfaction. The body experiences shock when they aren't present and begins to crave them intensely. Even though the cravings may be strong, you can overcome them. As your body adjusts to the new diet, eventually they go away on their own and you stop craving carbohydrates. However, initially overcoming the cravings can be challenging.

Can You Blend the Two?

Can the vegan and ketogenic diets be combined? The quick response is yes! The vegan keto diet will help you detox your body and get into incredible shape so that you feel your best. The long answer is that you can combine these two diets and enter ketosis without consuming any animal products, but you must be careful to consume enough plant-based protein. Even though it can be difficult, you can do it, and this book will show you how.

Getting your protein from plant sources is crucial. While fat does contribute to pushing your body into full ketosis, it represents a relatively small portion of the overall picture. Science has demonstrated that compared to fat, protein is actually much more nourishing and satisfying. Thus, obtaining protein is far more crucial than acquiring fat. This is good news for you if you're starting this diet because plants are rarely healthy sources of fat.

Some plants are still excellent sources of fat, though. Avocados, which have a significant amount of monounsaturated fat, would be one example. Plant oils are another source of fat. A vegan diet can still cause you to gain weight. In fact, MUFAs are incredibly beneficial sources of nutrition for reducing belly fat.

It may seem strange that consuming a specific type of fat can cause weight loss. But compared to other kinds of fat, like saturated fats, MUFAS operate quite differently. Without getting into complicated chemistry, this is because MUFAS provide good cholesterol without adding bad cholesterol, which helps your blood vessels maintain their shape. They aid in losing belly fat and lower the risk of heart disease. They essentially keep your body functioning and give you dense, calorie-dense energy that is ideal for the vegan keto diet. You can rely on foods high in MUFAS to meet your high fat requirements for the keto diet, but you should also eat foods high in protein to give you more energy.

Another thing to keep in mind is that maintaining a healthy lifestyle does not solely depend on diet. You must exercise if you want to be in the best possible shape. A good rule of thumb for staying in shape is to exercise for at least 30 minutes, three times per week (preferably more). Exercise is often thought to aid in weight loss, but this is a diet myth. By letting your muscles show, exercise will help you lose weight if you are also losing fat through diet. Exercise can help you build a lean or even muscular body, but it must be combined with a healthy diet. You won't typically be able to lose weight while exercising and eating a poor diet that keeps fat on your body. The keto diet and vegan diets, especially when combined, are great for promoting fat loss, so when combined with exercise, they will help you develop a fantastic physique.

Drinking enough water is also crucial. Make sure to drink at least 6 to 8 glasses of water each day if you're following this diet. It's also a good idea to mix powdered vegan electrolytes into your water, just make sure the supplement you pick doesn't have any added sugar. Avoid beverages with high sugar content, such as Gatorade, as they can cause your body to exit ketosis.

KETO VEGAN MAINS

Vegetarian Chickpea Tacos

Ingredients

- 2 (15 Oz.) cans chickpeas, drained and rinsed
- ¾ cups of water
- 1 (1 Oz.) package taco seasoning mix
- 8 taco shells

Directions

1. Put chickpeas on a medium heat in a pan. Taco seasoning and water are added. Cook and stir for 5 to 7 minutes, or until thoroughly heated. Get rid of the heat. Crush chickpeas by mashing the mixture.
2. Evenly distribute the chickpea filling among the taco shells.

Vegan Black Bean Quesadillas

Ingredients

- 1 (15 Oz.) can great Northern beans, drained and rinsed
- ¾ cups of diced tomatoes

- 1 clove garlic
- ⅓ cups of nutritional yeast
- 1 tsp. ground cumin
- ¼ tsp. chili powder
- salt to taste
- 1 pinch cayenne pepper, or to taste
- ½ cups of black beans, drained and rinsed
- ¼ cups of diced tomatoes
- 1 tbsp. olive oil, or as needed
- 8 whole grain tortillas
- cooking spray

Directions

1. Great Northern beans, 3/4 cups of tomatoes, garlic, and nutritional yeast should be processed in a food processor until smooth. Add salt, red pepper flakes, cumin, chili powder, and nutritional yeast, and process once more.
2. To a bowl, transfer the bean mixture. Add 1/4 cups of of tomatoes and black beans to the bean mixture.
3. In a skillet, heat the olive oil over medium-high heat.
4. In the hot oil, place a tortilla. Onto the tortilla, spoon about 1/4 cups of of the filling.
5. Another tortilla should be placed on top of the filling. Cook for 10 minutes, or until the filling is warmed.
6. Spray the top tortilla with cooking spray before flipping the quesadilla and cooking the other side for 3 to 5 minutes, until it is just lightly browned. Use the remaining tortillas and filling to repeat.

Jackfruit Vegan Tacos

Ingredients

- 2 (20 Oz.) cans jackfruit in brine - drained, rinsed, and cut into bite-sized pieces
- 1 tbsp. vegetable oil
- 1 tbsp. water, or more as needed
- 2 tbsp. taco seasoning mix, or to taste
- 4 taco shells
- ½ cups of salsa, or to taste

Directions

1. Oil is heated in a tiny pan over medium heat. After adding the jackfruit, stir-fry for 2 to 3 minutes. Taco seasoning and 1 tbsp. water are added; stir for 1 minute, or until thoroughly combined. Whenever more water is required, add 1 tbsp. at a time.
2. Each taco shell should contain a small amount of jackfruit and two tbsp. of salsa.

Vegan Air Fryer Taquitos

Ingredients

- 1 large russet potato, peeled

- 1 tsp. plant-based butter
- 2 tbsp. diced onions
- 1 clove garlic, minced
- ¼ cups of plant-based butter
- 2 tbsp. unsweetened, plain almond milk
- salt and ground black pepper to taste
- 6 corn tortillas
- avocado oil cooking spray

Directions

1. Put the potato in a pot and add salted water to cover; bring to a boil. Simmer for about 20 minutes until tender, then reduce heat to medium-low.
2. While the potatoes are boiling, soften 1 tsp. plant-based butter in a skillet and cook the onions for 3 to 5 minutes, or until they are translucent. Add the garlic and cook for about a minute, or until fragrant. Place aside
3. Drain the potato, then place it in a bowl. Add almond milk and 1/4 cups of vegan butter, season with salt and pepper, and mash. Garlic and onion should be thoroughly combined.
4. Tortillas should be heated until soft and pliable in a skillet or directly on the gas stove grates. Each tortilla should have 3 tbsp. of the potato mixture down the middle before being folded and rolled.
5. Achieve a 400°F air fryer temperature (200 degrees C).
6. Taquitos should not touch as they are placed in the air fryer basket. Avocado oil should then be misted over them. Whenever necessary, cook in batches.

7. Taquitos should be air-fried for 6 to 9 minutes or until golden brown and crispy. Taquitos should be turned over, sprayed with avocado oil, and air-fried for an additional 3 to 5 minutes.

Vegan Mexican Menudo

Ingredients

- 4 Roma tomatoes
- 2 ancho chile peppers, seeded and deveined
- 2 tbsp. olive oil
- 2 garlic cloves
- 1 pinch ground cumin
- 2 lbs shiitake mushrooms, sliced
- ½ cups of water
- salt to taste
- 1 quart vegetable broth
- Garnish:
- ¼ cups of finely chopped white onion
- ¼ tsp. dried oregano
- 1 lime, cut in wedges
- 1 tsp. red pepper flakes

Directions

1. In a pot, combine the tomatoes and ancho peppers; add the water; and bring to a boil. Cook for about 5 minutes, or until

the vegetables are tender. Give the soak five more minutes in the hot water.

2. Add 1/2 cups of of water, tomatoes, and ancho peppers to a blender. With a potholder, cover the container and secure the lid. Pulse the food a few times before blending. Sauce should be passed through a sieve with the solids removed.
3. Oil is heated in a pan at medium heat. In a bowl, combine the cumin and garlic and crush. Add to the hot pan. For about a minute, cook and stir until fragrant. Add the mushrooms and stir-fry for 5 minutes or until soft. Add salt and tomato sauce to the mushroom mixture. Allow sauce to simmer for 5 minutes or until it slightly thickens. Including vegetable broth up to a boil. Reduce heat and simmer soup for 15 minutes or until flavors are blended.
4. Place soup in individual bowls and top with oregano and onion. Red pepper flakes and lime wedges should be served on the side.

Vegan Fajitas

Ingredients

Marinade:

- ¼ cups of olive oil
- ¼ cups of red wine vinegar
- 1 tsp. dried oregano
- 1 tsp. chili powder

- 1 tsp. white sugar
- garlic salt to taste
- salt and pepper to taste

Fajitas:

- 2 small zucchini, julienned
- 2 medium small yellow squash, julienned
- 1 large onion, sliced
- 1 green bell pepper, cut into thin strips
- 1 red bell pepper, cut into thin strips
- 2 tbsp. olive oil
- 1 (8.75 Oz.) can whole kernel corn, drained
- 1 (15 Oz.) can black beans, drained

Directions

1. Creating the marinade In a sizable bowl, mix the olive oil, vinegar, oregano, chili powder, sugar, garlic salt, salt, and pepper.
2. Making fajitas: Bell peppers, onion, zucchini, and yellow squash can all be added to the marinade. Vegetables should be marinated in the fridge for no more than 24 hours, but at least for 30 minutes.
3. In a sizable skillet, heat the oil over medium-high heat. Vegetables should be drained and sautéed for 10 to 15 minutes, or until tender. Add corn and black beans and stir. For about 5 minutes, raise the heat to high in order to brown the vegetables.

Vegan Tacos al Pastor

Ingredients

Filling:

- 5 guajillo chile peppers, stemmed and seeded
- 5 limes, juiced
- 2 cloves garlic
- 2 pinches ground cumin
- 3 whole cloves
- 2 cups of water, divided
- 2 tbsp. vegetable oil
- ½ onion, halved and cut into thin slices
- 1 ½ (12 Oz.) packages textured vegetable protein

Salsa:

- 4 tomatoes
- 4 dried chile de arbol peppers, stemmed
- 1 slice onion
- 1 clove garlic
- salt to taste
- 1 (32 Oz.) package corn tortillas

Garnish:

- 1 large onion, chopped
- 1 bunch cilantro, finely chopped

Directions

1. In a saucepan, add the guajillo peppers and cover with water. Boil for 10 minutes, or until the peppers are soft. Drain.
2. In a small saucepan over medium heat, combine the lime juice, 2 cloves of garlic, cumin, and cloves; bring to a boil. After five minutes, remove from the heat. Guajillo peppers should be added to the liquid before blending until smooth. If the sauce is too thick, add 1 to 2 tbsp. of water.
3. Onion slices should be cooked in hot oil for about 5 minutes, or until they are soft and translucent. After adding the vegetable protein, stir continuously for 2 minutes. Add the remaining water and guajillo sauce, then salt to taste. Bring to a boil; lower heat to medium-low; cook, covered, for 10 minutes or until flavors are blended.
4. Heat up the oven's broiler while positioning the oven rack about 6 inches from the heat source. In a baking dish, mix tomatoes and chile de arbol peppers.
5. For 5 to 10 minutes, roast the tomatoes and peppers until they are charred. a little tomato cooling Peel.
6. Blend the tomatoes, peppers, onion, garlic, one clove, and salt in a blender until smooth. Place salsa in a tiny bowl.
7. Corn tortillas are warmed in a skillet. Top each tortilla with a portion of the vegetable protein mixture, chopped onion, and cilantro, and serve.

Vegan Mexican Quinoa Bowl with Green Chile Cilantro Sauce

Ingredients

Vegan Green Chile Cilantro Sauce:

- 1 cups of unsalted raw cashews
- 1 (4 Oz.) can chopped green chile peppers
- ¼ cups of hemp milk
- ½ jalapeno pepper with seeds, or more to taste
- ½ tsp. salt
- 1 ¼ cups of chopped fresh cilantro
- 3 cups of water
- 1 ½ cups of quinoa
- 2 romaine hearts, chopped
- 2 (15 Oz.) cans black beans, rinsed and drained
- 3 cups of chopped red bell pepper
- ½ cups of chopped red onion
- 2 avocados, chopped

Directions

1. Blend the cashews, salt, jalapeno pepper, green chile peppers, hemp milk, and other ingredients until smooth.
2. Fill a small bowl with the cashew mixture and top with 1 cups of of cilantro.
3. In a saucepan, bring water and quinoa to a boil. Reduce heat to medium-low, cover, and simmer for 15 to 20 minutes, or until quinoa is tender.
4. 4 bowls should each contain some romaine lettuce. Quinoa, black beans, red bell pepper, and onion should be added on top. On top, drizzle some cilantro sauce. Avocados and the final 1/4 cups of of cilantro are used as garnish.

Plant-Based Black Bean Taco Soup

Ingredients

- 2 tbsp. grapeseed oil
- 1 medium onion, chopped
- 1 medium green bell pepper, cut into bite-sized pieces
- 1 medium red bell pepper, cut into bite-sized pieces
- 2 stalks celery, chopped
- 2 medium carrots, chopped
- 2 medium jalapeno peppers, seeded and minced
- 4 cloves garlic, chopped
- 2 (14.5 Oz.) cans fire-roasted diced tomatoes
- 1 (32 fluid Oz.) container vegetable broth
- 2 (15 Oz.) cans black beans, rinsed and drained
- 1 (15 Oz.) can pinto beans, rinsed and drained
- ¼ cups of frozen corn
- ½ tsp. ground cumin, or to taste
- ¼ tsp. chili powder, or to taste
- ¼ tsp. smoked paprika, or to taste
- salt to taste

Directions

1. In a Dutch oven, heat the oil over medium heat. Add the garlic, onion, bell peppers, celery, carrots, and jalapeno peppers; cook for 3 to 5 minutes, or until the vegetables soften.

2. After thoroughly stirring for three minutes, add the diced tomatoes. Stir in the black and pinto beans, corn, cumin, chili powder, paprika, and salt after adding the vegetable broth. Simmer for 30 minutes with cover on, medium-low heat.

Vegan Sweet Potato and Bean Burritos

Ingredients

- 1 cups of sweet potato, peeled and cut into 1/4-inch cubes
- ½ cups of yellow onion, sliced
- 2 tbsp. olive oil
- 1 tbsp. taco seasoning mix
- ½ cups of vegan refried beans
- 4 large vegan tortillas
- 1 cups of cooked brown rice
- ¼ cups of salsa

Directions

1. Set the oven to 450 degrees Fahrenheit (230 degrees C).
2. In a bowl, combine sweet potatoes, onion, olive oil, and taco seasoning. Onto a baking sheet, spread out.
3. Roast for about 30 minutes, or until desired degree of doneness, in the preheated oven.
4. Each tortilla should have 1/4 of the beans down the middle. Add 1/4 cups of rice, 1/4 of the vegetable mixture, and 1 tbsp. salsa to the top of each tortilla.

Easy Vegan Chili

Ingredients

- 3 tbsp. olive oil
- 1 onion, chopped
- 2 cloves garlic, minced
- 1 large baking potato, peeled and cut into 1/2-inch cubes
- 1 cups of dry red lentils
- 4 cups of vegetable broth
- 2 (15 Oz.) cans kidney beans, rinsed and drained
- 1 (15.25 Oz.) can whole kernel corn, drained
- 4 cups of tomato puree
- 1 tbsp. ground sweet paprika
- 1 tsp. spicy chili powder
- salt and freshly cracked black pepper to taste
- 1 pinch white sugar
- 1 bunch fresh chives, chopped

Directions

1. In a pot with medium heat, cook the onion for about 5 minutes, until it becomes soft and translucent. Add the garlic and cook for 30 seconds or until fragrant. Cook the potato for 3 to 5 minutes after adding. Add lentils and stir. After adding the vegetable broth, simmer it for 20 minutes. Add tomato puree, corn, and kidney beans. Bring to a boil; then, turn down the

heat, cover the pan, and simmer for 10 minutes to let the flavors meld. Add paprika, chili powder, sugar, salt, and pepper for seasoning.

2. In four bowls, distribute the chili and top with chives.

Ginger Veggie Stir-Fry

Ingredients

- 4 tbsp. vegetable oil, divided
- 2 tsp. chopped fresh ginger root, divided
- 1 ½ cloves garlic, crushed
- 1 tbsp. cornstarch
- 1 small head broccoli, cut into florets
- ¾ cups of julienned carrots
- ½ cups of snow peas
- ½ cups of halved green beans
- 2 ½ tbsp. water
- 2 tbsp. soy sauce
- ¼ cups of chopped onion
- ½ tbsp. salt

Directions

1. In a large bowl, combine 2 tbsp. vegetable oil, 1 tsp. each of ginger, garlic, and cornstarch. Stir until the cornstarch is completely dissolved. Add the green beans, broccoli, carrots, snow peas, and toss to coat.

2. In a big skillet or wok, heat the last 2 tbsp. of vegetable oil on medium. Stirring continuously for 2 minutes to prevent burning, add the vegetable mixture.
3. Add onion, salt, and the final 1 tsp. of ginger; stir in water and soy sauce. Cook and stir the vegetables until they are crisp and tender.

Vegan Enchilada Bake

Ingredients

- 1 cups of crushed tomatoes
- 2 cups of cooked white rice
- 1 (15 Oz.) can vegetarian refried beans
- ½ (16 Oz.) can diced tomatoes and green chiles
- 8 Oz. sliced seitan
- ½ (8 Oz.) package shredded mozzarella-style vegan cheese
- 9 (6 inch) corn tortillas
- 1 (15 Oz.) can green enchilada sauce

Directions

1. Set the oven to 350 degrees Fahrenheit (175 degrees C).
2. Crushed tomatoes should be poured into a casserole dish's base. In that order, add 1/3 each of the following ingredients to the dish: 1/3 of the rice, 1/3 of the beans, 1/3 of the diced tomatoes, 1/3 of the seitan, 1/3 of the vegan cheese, 1/3 of the

tortillas, and 1/3 of the enchilada sauce. Add two more layers and repeat.
3. Bake for about 45 minutes, or until vegan cheese melts and casserole is thoroughly heated.

Vegetarian Chickpea Tacos

Ingredients

- 2 (15 Oz.) cans chickpeas, drained and rinsed
- ¾ cups of water
- 1 (1 Oz.) package taco seasoning mix
- 8 taco shells

Directions

1. Put chickpeas on a medium heat in a pan. Taco seasoning and water are added. Cook and stir for 5 to 7 minutes, or until thoroughly heated. Get rid of the heat. Crush chickpeas by mashing the mixture.
2. Evenly distribute the chickpea filling among the taco shells.

Spicy Vegan Potato Curry

Ingredients

- 4 potatoes, peeled and cubed
- 2 tbsp. vegetable oil
- 1 yellow onion, diced
- 3 cloves garlic, minced
- 2 tsp. ground cumin
- 1 ½ tsp. cayenne pepper
- 4 tsp. curry powder
- 4 tsp. garam masala
- 1 (1 inch) piece fresh ginger root, peeled and minced
- 2 tsp. salt
- 1 (14.5 Oz.) can diced tomatoes
- 1 (15 Oz.) can garbanzo beans, rinsed and drained
- 1 (15 Oz.) can peas, drained
- 1 (14 Oz.) can coconut milk

Directions

1. Add salty water to a large pot and add the potatoes. Over high heat, bring to a boil; then, lower the heat to medium-low, cover, and simmer for about 15 minutes, or until the food is just tender. Drain and let steam dry for one or two minutes.
2. In the meantime, preheat a big skillet with the vegetable oil over medium heat. Add the onion and garlic, stirring constantly, and cook and stir for about 5 minutes, or until the onion has softened and become translucent. Add salt, cumin, ginger, cayenne pepper, curry powder, garam masala, and curry; cook for an additional two minutes. Potatoes, tomatoes, garbanzo beans, and peas should all be added. Add the coconut milk, then simmer the mixture. Prior to serving, simmer for 5 to 10 minutes.

Simple Vegan Split Pea Soup

Ingredients

- 1 cups of dried split peas
- 5 cups of cold water
- ¼ cups of diced onion
- ¼ cups of thinly sliced celery
- 1 tbsp. ketchup
- 1 tbsp. extra-virgin olive oil
- 1 pinch coarse salt
- 2 cloves garlic, crushed, or more to taste
- 3 bay leaves, or more to taste
- 1 cups of sliced carrots, or more to taste
- ground black pepper to taste

Directions

1. Remove any stones, foreign objects, or ugly peas after inspecting the crop. To get rid of pea dust, put the peas in a strainer with fine mesh and run cold water over them.
2. Put the drained peas in a lidded pot with a thick, heat-diffusing bottom. Include water, ketchup, ketchup, onion, celery, salt, garlic, and bay leaves. Over medium-high heat, cover and bring to a boil. Turn down the heat to a simmer. Cook for approximately 1 1/2 hours, stirring and scraping the bottom

every 7 to 12 minutes, or until the peas have mostly broken apart.

3. Add carrots to the soup and stir. Cook for an additional 1 1/2 hours, covered and stirring frequently, or until the soup is thick. Remove and throw away the bay leaves. Use pepper to season.

Tofu and Veggies in Peanut Sauce

Ingredients

- 1 tbsp. peanut oil
- 1 small head broccoli, chopped
- 1 small red bell pepper, chopped
- 5 fresh mushrooms, sliced
- 1 lb firm tofu, cubed
- ½ cups of peanut butter
- ½ cups of hot water
- 2 tbsp. vinegar
- 2 tbsp. soy sauce
- 1 ½ tbsp. molasses
- ground cayenne pepper to taste

Directions

1. In a sizable skillet or wok, heat the oil over medium-high heat. For five minutes, saute broccoli, red bell pepper, mushrooms, and tofu.

2. Mix the peanut butter, hot water, vinegar, soy sauce, molasses, and cayenne pepper in a small bowl. Pour over the tofu and vegetables. Vegetables should be tender crisp after 3 to 5 minutes of simmering.

Chickpea Buddha Bowl

Ingredients

- 1 cups of vegetable broth
- ½ cups of red quinoa
- 1 ¾ cups of Brussels sprouts
- ¼ cups of cubed carrots
- ¼ cups of peeled and cubed parsnips
- ½ red onion, chopped
- 2 tsp. olive oil, divided
- 1 (15 Oz.) can chickpeas, drained and patted dry
- 1 tsp. ground turmeric

Dressing:

- ¼ cups of tahini
- 2 tbsp. lemon juice
- 1 tbsp. maple syrup
- 5 tbsp. hot water
- 1 avocado, mashed

Directions

1. Set oven to 400 degrees Fahrenheit (200 degrees C).
2. In a saucepan, combine the quinoa and vegetable broth. Bring to a boil. For about 15 minutes, simmer the quinoa until it is tender.
3. On a baking sheet, arrange the Brussels sprouts, carrots, parsnips, and red onion. Drizzle with the olive oil.
4. For about 10 minutes, bake in the preheated oven until soft.
5. In a bowl, combine chickpeas and turmeric. In a skillet, warm the last tsp. of olive oil over medium heat. For about 8 minutes, cook and stir chickpeas until they are browned.
6. Tahini, lemon juice, and maple syrup should all be thoroughly combined in a bowl. One tbsp. at a time, add hot water to make dressing thin and smooth.
7. In two serving bowls, distribute the quinoa, roasted vegetables, chickpeas, and mashed avocado. Give each bowl a tbsp. of dressing.

Vegan Stir-Fry

Ingredients

- 2 tbsp. canola oil
- 1 small onion, diced
- 1 clove garlic, minced
- ½ cups of sliced carrots
- ½ cups of purple cauliflower, chopped
- ½ cups of chopped fresh broccoli florets

- ½ cups of sliced fresh mushrooms
- 4 tbsp. soy sauce
- ¾ cups of water
- 1 cups of cherry tomatoes, halved
- salt and freshly ground black pepper to taste
- 1 tbsp. fresh basil, chopped, or to taste
- 2 cups of cooked rice
- 1 tsp. toasted sesame seeds

Directions

1. Over medium heat, add oil to a large skillet, and cook onion for about 4 minutes, or until soft and translucent. Add the garlic and cook for 30 seconds or until fragrant. Carrots, cauliflower, broccoli, and mushrooms should be added last, and each addition should be sauteed for about two minutes. Add the soy sauce and stir until the sauce is evenly distributed throughout the vegetables. For two minutes, cook.
2. Tomatoes, salt, and pepper are added after adding water. Bring to a boil, then turn down the heat and simmer. Cook for 3 to 5 minutes, or until all vegetables are fork-tender but not overly soft. Near the end, add the basil.
3. Serve warm over rice that has been dusted with sesame seeds.

Lentil Rice and Veggie Bake

Ingredients

- ½ cups of uncooked long grain white rice
- 2 ½ cups of water
- 1 cups of red lentils
- 1 tsp. vegetable oil
- 1 small onion, chopped
- 3 cloves garlic, minced
- 1 fresh tomato, chopped
- ⅓ cups of chopped celery
- ⅓ cups of chopped carrots
- ⅓ cups of chopped zucchini
- 1 (8 Oz.) can tomato sauce
- 1 tsp. dried basil
- 1 tsp. dried oregano
- 1 tsp. ground cumin
- salt and pepper to taste

Directions

1. Bring to a boil 1 cups of of water and the rice in a pot. For 20 minutes, simmer with the lid on and the heat on low. Bring the remaining 1 1/2 cups of of water to a boil in a pot with the lentils. 15 minutes of cooking time or until tender.
2. Set oven to 350 degrees Fahrenheit (175 degrees C).
3. The onion and garlic are added to the oil as it is heating in a skillet over medium heat. Add tomato, 1/2 the tomato sauce, celery, carrots, and zucchini to the mixture. Add salt, pepper, and half of the basil, oregano, and cumin to season. Cook the vegetables until they are soft.

4. Combine the rice, lentils, and vegetables in a casserole dish. Sprinkle the remaining basil, oregano, and cumin on top before adding the remaining tomato sauce.
5. Bake for 30 minutes, or until bubbly, in a preheated oven.

Vegan Mac and No Cheese

Ingredients

- 1 (8 Oz.) package uncooked elbow macaroni
- 1 tbsp. vegetable oil
- 1 medium onion, chopped
- 1 cups of cashews
- ⅓ cups of lemon juice
- 1 ⅓ cups of water
- salt to taste
- ⅓ cups of canola oil
- 4 Oz. roasted red peppers, drained
- 3 tbsp. nutritional yeast
- 1 tsp. garlic powder
- 1 tsp. onion powder

Directions

1. Set oven to 350 degrees Fahrenheit (175 degrees C).
2. Large pot of lightly salted water should be brought to a boil. Drain the macaroni after cooking for 8 to 10 minutes, or until it is al dente. To a medium baking dish, transfer.

3. In a medium saucepan set over medium heat, warm the vegetable oil. Add onion and stir. Cook until onion is soft and barely browned. Mix the macaroni gently.
4. Salt, water, lemon juice, and cashews should all be combined in a blender or food processor. Blend in the nutritional yeast, roasted red peppers, canola oil, garlic powder, and onion powder gradually. Until smooth, blend. Mix the macaroni and onions thoroughly.
5. Bake for 45 minutes, or until the top is just beginning to brown. ten to fifteen minutes to cool before serving.

Vegan Baked Polenta with Radicchio

Ingredients

- 3 tsp. olive oil, divided
- 1 ½ cups of vegetable broth
- 1 ½ cups of water, divided
- ¾ cups of unsweetened oat milk
- 1 ½ cups of medium grind, whole-grain cornmeal
- ½ cups of sliced yellow onion
- ½ cups of shredded carrot
- 1 medium head radicchio, cored and thinly sliced
- ½ tsp. coarse ground black pepper
- ½ tsp. ground turmeric
- 3 (1 Oz.) slices vegan smoked Gouda
- 3 ½ Oz. vegan shredded mozzarella

Directions

1. Set the oven to 355 degrees Fahrenheit (180 degrees C). 1 tsp. of olive oil should be used to grease an 8x8 baking dish.
2. Large pot over high heat, add vegetable broth and 1 cups of of water, and bring to a boil. Turn down the heat to medium, maintaining a low boil. Add unsweetened oat milk and heat until boiling. Add the cornmeal while whisking continuously to prevent clumps from forming. Medium-low heat should be used, and stirring should continue until the polenta starts to thicken. When necessary, add more water. About 20 minutes of stirring is required for the polenta to soften and thicken.
3. In the interim, warm the final 2 tsp. of olive oil in a skillet. Include carrot and onion. Saute the vegetables until they are just starting to soften. Add the radicchio and cook it until it wilts. Add pepper and turmeric for seasoning. Cook for about 5 minutes, or until vegetables are completely cooked and tender.
4. Half of the polenta should be spread out in the greased baking dish. On top, evenly distribute half of the vegan mozzarella and half of the vegan Gouda. Add half of the radicchio mixture on top. With the remaining polenta, cheeses, and radicchio mixture, repeat the layering.
5. For about 20 minutes, or until the cheese is bubbling and melted, bake in the preheated oven. 5 minutes should pass before serving.

Vegan Romanian Eggplant Bake

Ingredients

- 3 eggplants
- 4 cups of vegetable broth
- 3 tbsp. olive oil
- 4 red bell peppers, cut into cubes
- 2 onions, chopped
- 2 cloves garlic, sliced
- salt and freshly ground black pepper
- 3 tomatoes, sliced

Directions

1. Peel the eggplants so that each one has 3 strips of skin still attached. Peeled eggplant should be cut into 1/2-inch slices. The skin strips will stop the cooked eggplant slices from disintegrating as they cook.
2. Slices of eggplant are cooked for one minute in batches after being added to boiling vegetable broth in a big pot. Pour into a sieve, then thoroughly drain.
3. Set oven to 375 degrees Fahrenheit (190 degrees C). Use 1 tbsp. of olive oil to grease a sizable baking dish. The bottom of the baking dish should be covered with eggplant slices.
4. Bell peppers, onions, and garlic should be cooked in the remaining 2 tbsp. of olive oil in a large skillet over medium heat for 5 to 10 minutes, or until soft. Sprinkle salt and pepper over the eggplant before seasoning. Slices of tomato should be added after salt and pepper.
5. Vegetables should be baked in the preheated oven for 20 to 30 minutes or until tender.

Vegan Shepherd's Pie with Sweet Potato

Ingredients

- 1 tbsp. coconut oil
- 1 red onion, chopped
- 1 white onion, chopped
- 1 tbsp. ground cinnamon
- 1 tbsp. grated fresh ginger root
- 2 cloves garlic, chopped
- 2 tsp. cumin, divided
- 3 cups of cooked lentils
- 1 (14 Oz.) can chopped tomatoes
- 1 ½ cups of vegetable stock
- 1 tbsp. maple syrup
- 2 ½ sweet potatoes, peeled and chopped, or to taste
- ⅓ cups of coconut milk
- 1 tbsp. nutritional yeast, or to taste

Directions

1. Set the oven to 350 degrees Fahrenheit (175 degrees C).
2. In a saucepan, heat the coconut oil over medium-high heat. Add 1 tsp. each of cumin, cinnamon, ginger, and white and red onions. Cook for about 5 minutes while gently stirring, until soft and tender. Add the stock, maple syrup, tomatoes, and

lentils. Bring to a boil, then simmer the filling for 20 to 30 minutes to blend the flavors.

3. To boil, add salted water to a large pot with the sweet potatoes inside. Simmer for about 20 minutes until softened, reducing heat to medium-low. Drain the water, then give the sweet potatoes coconut milk and the final tsp. of cumin. until smooth, mash.
4. Filling should be poured into a sizable baking dish. Sweet potato mash and nutritional yeast should then be added on top.
5. Bake in the preheated oven for about 20 minutes, or until the top is browned.

Vegan Enchilada Bake

Ingredients

- 1 cups of crushed tomatoes
- 2 cups of cooked white rice
- 1 (15 Oz.) can vegetarian refried beans
- ½ (16 Oz.) can diced tomatoes and green chiles
- 8 Oz. sliced seitan
- ½ (8 Oz.) package shredded mozzarella-style vegan cheese
- 9 (6 inch) corn tortillas
- 1 (15 Oz.) can green enchilada sauce

Directions

1. Set the oven to 350 degrees Fahrenheit (175 degrees C).

2. Crushed tomatoes should be poured into a casserole dish's base. In that order, add 1/3 each of the following ingredients to the dish: 1/3 of the rice, 1/3 of the beans, 1/3 of the diced tomatoes, 1/3 of the seitan, 1/3 of the vegan cheese, 1/3 of the tortillas, and 1/3 of the enchilada sauce. Add two more layers and repeat.
3. Bake for about 45 minutes, or until vegan cheese melts and casserole is thoroughly heated.

Vegan Black Bean Soup

Ingredients

- 1 tbsp. olive oil
- 1 large onion, chopped
- 2 carrots, chopped
- 1 stalk celery, chopped
- 4 cloves garlic, chopped
- 2 tbsp. chili powder
- 1 tbsp. ground cumin
- 1 pinch black pepper
- 4 cups of vegetable broth
- 4 (15 Oz.) cans black beans, undrained, divided
- 1 (15 Oz.) can whole kernel corn
- 1 (14.5 Oz.) can crushed tomatoes

Directions

1. Oil in a big pot is heated up over medium-high heat. For five minutes, sauté the onion, carrots, celery, and garlic. Cook for one minute after seasoning with cumin, black pepper, and chili powder. Add the corn, two cans of beans, and vegetable broth. up to a boil.
2. In the meantime, blend or food process the remaining 2 cans of beans and tomatoes until they are smooth. Stir into the simmering soup mixture after it has reached a rolling boil.

Vegan Kale and Chickpea Soup

Ingredients

- cooking spray
- 1 tsp. minced garlic
- ¼ cups of minced onion
- 1 quart vegetable broth, divided
- 4 cups of chopped kale leaves
- 1 (15 Oz.) can chickpeas, drained and rinsed
- 1 cube vegetable bouillon
- ¼ tsp. curry powder
- 1 cups of almond milk

Directions

1. Cooking spray the interior of a stockpot, then set it over medium heat. For 2 to 3 minutes, cook and stir the garlic in the stockpot until it is just starting to brown. Add onion and

roughly 2 tbsp. of vegetable broth to the garlic; cook and stir for 5 to 10 minutes, or until the onion is translucent.

2. Add the kale to the onion mixture and cook for 3 to 4 minutes, until just starting to wilt. Bring to a boil the chickpeas, remaining vegetable broth, vegetable bouillon, and curry powder. Reduce heat, cover, and simmer for 15 minutes or until thoroughly heated. Cook for 2 to 3 minutes, stirring occasionally, after adding the almond milk.

Vegan Chickpea Noodle Soup

Ingredients

- 2 tbsp. olive oil
- 3 large carrots, diced
- 3 stalks celery, diced
- 1 large yellow onion, diced
- 5 cloves garlic, minced
- 12 cups of vegetable broth
- 2 tsp. herbes de Provence
- 3 dried bay leaves
- ½ tsp. ground black pepper, or more to taste
- 1 (12 Oz.) package wide vegan noodles
- 2 (15 Oz.) cans chickpeas, drained and rinsed
- ½ cups of chopped fresh parsley
- 1 tbsp. fresh lemon juice

Directions

1. Over medium-high heat, warm the olive oil in a big, heavy pot. Add the carrots, celery, and onion and cook, stirring only occasionally, for about 10 minutes, or until the vegetables are beginning to soften. Add the garlic and cook for another minute.
2. Bring the broth, herbs de Provence, bay leaves, and black pepper to a boil in the pot with the vegetables. 10 minutes of covered simmering.
3. While the broth is simmering, heat up a pot of salted water to a boil, and cook the noodles for 7 minutes or as directed on the package, until they are tender but still firm to the bite. Noodles should be drained and tossed with a little oil to avoid sticking.
4. After removing the soup from the heat, add the parsley, lemon juice, and chickpeas. Pour soup into bowls and, just before serving, top each bowl with noodles.

Vegan Black Bean Burger Soup

Ingredients

- 2 tbsp. olive oil
- 1 medium onion, diced
- 2 stalks celery, chopped
- 3 cloves garlic, minced
- 3 tbsp. tomato paste

- 1 tsp. ground mustard powder
- ½ tsp. salt
- ½ tsp. ground white pepper
- 1 (32 fluid Oz.) container vegetable broth
- 2 medium sweet potatoes, cut into 1/2-inch cubes
- 1 (15 Oz.) can low-sodium black beans, rinsed and drained
- 1 (10 Oz.) bag plant-based "ground beef" ½ (8 Oz.) package fresh baby spinach
- 3 tbsp. nutritional yeast

Directions

1. In a medium stockpot, heat the olive oil over medium-high heat. For about 5 minutes, add the onion, celery, and garlic and saute until soft. Add salt, pepper, mustard powder, and tomato paste. Sweet potatoes should also be added. Covered, bring to a boil. Cook potatoes for about 6 minutes, stirring occasionally, until they are tender.
2. Add nutritional yeast, spinach, black beans, and vegan "ground beef," then turn the heat down to low. Cook for about 10 minutes, or until spinach has softened and soup is thoroughly heated.

Vegetarian Kale Soup

Ingredients

- 2 tbsp. olive oil

- 1 yellow onion, chopped
- 2 tbsp. chopped garlic
- 1 bunch kale, stems removed and leaves chopped
- 8 cups of water
- 6 white potatoes, peeled and cubed
- 2 (15 Oz.) cans cannellini beans
- 1 (15 Oz.) can diced tomatoes
- 6 cubes vegetable bouillon
- 2 tbsp. dried parsley
- 1 tbsp. Italian seasoning
- salt and pepper to taste

Directions

1. Onion and garlic should be cooked in olive oil for 2 to 3 minutes, until they are soft. Add the kale and stir, cooking for 2 minutes or until wilted. Add the water, vegetable bouillon, parsley, Italian seasoning, potatoes, beans, and tomatoes.
2. Bring to a boil, then lower the heat and simmer for about 25 minutes, or until the potatoes are tender. Add salt and pepper to taste.

Quick Vegan Veggie Sandwich

Ingredients

- 1 tbsp. extra-virgin olive oil
- 1 small garlic clove, finely chopped

- ½ small tomato, finely chopped
- ¼ green bell pepper, finely chopped
- ¼ red onion, finely chopped
- salt and ground black pepper to taste
- 2 slices multigrain bread
- 1 tbsp. hummus spread
- 1 tbsp. vegan mayonnaise
- salt and ground black pepper to taste
- 4 sun-dried tomatoes packed in oil, drained and chopped
- 2 leaves lettuce, or more to taste

Directions

1. For one minute, cook garlic and olive oil in a frying pan at medium heat. Add tomato, onion, and bell pepper. Cook for 4 minutes or until soft. Add salt and pepper, then turn off the heat.
2. Toast a few slices of bread while the vegetables are cooking. On one slice, spread hummus. On the opposite, spread vegan mayonnaise and sprinkle with salt and pepper.
3. On one slice, arrange lettuce, cooked vegetables, and sun-dried tomatoes. Cover with the second slice. Half the sandwich.

Easy Vegan Lemon Cake

Ingredients

- baking spray

- 2 ¼ cups of all-purpose flour
- 1 tsp. baking powder
- 1 tsp. baking soda
- ½ tsp. salt
- 1 ½ cups of white sugar
- ⅔ cups of margarine, melted
- ⅔ cups of soy milk
- ½ cups of soy yogurt
- ½ cups of lemon juice
- 2 tbsp. lemon zest
- 2 tsp. vanilla extract

Directions

1. Set the oven to 350 degrees Fahrenheit (175 degrees C). Two 9-inch round cake pans should be sprayed with baking spray.
2. In a bowl, combine the flour, salt, baking soda, and baking powder.
3. In a sizable bowl, combine the sugar, margarine, soy milk, and soy yogurt. Add vanilla and the lemon juice and zest. Two batches at a time, whisking well after each addition of the flour mixture. Evenly distribute the batter among the prepared pans.
4. Bake in the preheated oven for 32 to 35 minutes, or until a toothpick or knife inserted in the center comes out clean.
5. For 5 minutes, let cakes cool in their pans on a wire rack. To loosen, go around the edges with a table knife. Carefully invert onto a cooling rack. Allow 30 minutes for the frosting to completely cool.

Grilled Asparagus

Ingredients

- 1 lb fresh asparagus spears, trimmed
- 1 tbsp. olive oil
- salt and pepper to taste

Directions

1. Get the grill ready for high heat.
2. Olive oil should be lightly applied to the asparagus spears. To taste, add salt and pepper to the food.
3. Grill for 2 to 3 minutes on high, or until desired tenderness is reached.

Easy Vegan Cinnamon Rolls

Ingredients

Dough:

- 6 ½ tbsp. white sugar
- 5 ½ tbsp. vegetable shortening
- 1 tsp. salt
- 2 tbsp. applesauce
- 1 tbsp. cornstarch
- 1 tsp. lemon juice

- 3 ½ cups of all-purpose flour
- 1 ¼ cups of soy milk
- 1 (.25 Oz.) package instant yeast

Filling:

- 6 ½ tbsp. white sugar
- 1 ½ tbsp. ground cinnamon

Icing:

- ½ cups of powdered sugar
- 1 tsp. soy milk
- ¼ tsp. vanilla extract

Directions

1. Salt, shortening, and sugar are combined in a cream. Add cornstarch, lemon juice, and applesauce and blend until smooth. Till dough comes together, combine yeast, flour, and soy milk.
2. For several minutes, knead the dough on a floured surface. After that, let it rise for about two hours in an oiled, covered bowl.
3. About the size of a cookie sheet, roll out the dough into a rectangle. The dough should be covered with the filling, which you should use all of even though it may seem like a lot. Combine the sugar and cinnamon.
4. Keep the loose end of each roll on the bottom as you cut the dough into six rolls after rolling it up into a cylinder. Rolls should rise on a baking sheet covered with parchment paper for 1 to 1 1/2 hours or until they have doubled in size.

5. Set the oven to 350 degrees Fahrenheit (175 degrees C).
6. Bake for 20 to 30 minutes, or until golden, in a preheated oven.
7. Prepare the icing by combining powdered sugar, milk, and vanilla in a bowl while the rolls are baking.
8. Take the rolls out of the oven. After allowing to cool for about 10 minutes, top with icing. Serve hot!

Spicy Vegan Lasagna

Ingredients

Lasagna:

- 1 (16 Oz.) package lasagna noodles

Filling:

- 1 (12 Oz.) package vegetarian burger crumbles
- 2 links vegetarian Italian-style sausage, diced, or more as needed
- 4 meatless meatballs, crumbled, or more as needed
- 1 yellow squash, diced
- 2 carrots, diced
- 1 small yellow onion, diced
- 3 whole mushrooms, diced
- 1 portobello mushroom, diced
- 2 tbsp. olive oil, or as needed
- 2 cloves garlic, minced
- ½ tsp. garlic powder, or to taste

- ½ tsp. ground black pepper, or to taste
- ½ tsp. dried oregano, or to taste
- ½ tsp. dried thyme, or to taste
- ¼ tsp. fennel seed, or to taste

Sauce:

- 1 (26 Oz.) jar marinara sauce
- 1 (10 Oz.) can diced tomatoes with green chile peppers

Directions

1. Set the oven to 375 degrees Fahrenheit (190 degrees C).
2. Lightly salted water should be added to a large pot and brought to a rolling boil. Add lasagna and bring back to a boil. Cook uncovered for about 8 minutes, stirring occasionally, until fork-tender but still firm.
3. Mix the crumbles, sausage, meatballs, squash, carrots, onions, mushrooms, oil, garlic powder, pepper, oregano, thyme, and fennel in a big bowl while the noodles are cooking. In a separate bowl, mix the diced tomatoes and marinara sauce.
4. Delete pasta. Use olive oil to grease a 9x13-inch baking dish. On the bottom, smear a thin layer of sauce. Repeat the layering process once more, starting with 1 layer of lasagna noodles, a thin layer of sauce, 1/2 of the filling, and about 4 tbsp. sauce. Lay the final layer of lasagna noodles on top, then ladle plenty of sauce on top of that. Use aluminum foil to cover the dish.
5. Bake for 30 to 40 minutes in a preheated oven, or until thoroughly cooked.

Vegan Vanilla Cake

Ingredients

- 2 ⅓ cups of cake flour
- 1 ½ cups of white sugar
- 1 tbsp. baking powder
- ¾ tsp. salt
- 3 tsp. dry egg replacer
- ¼ cups of warm water
- 1 cups of soy milk
- ½ cups of vegetable oil
- 1 tsp. vanilla extract

Directions

1. Set the oven to 350 degrees Fahrenheit (175 degrees C). A 9-inch round cake pan should be greased and floured.
2. Sift the following ingredients into a sizable bowl: cake flour, sugar, baking soda, and salt.
3. In a small bowl, combine warm water and dry egg substitute. To the dry ingredients, add the egg replacement mixture, soy milk, oil, and vanilla. For one minute, use a low speed electric mixer. Increasing the speed to high, beat for two minutes while frequently scraping the bowl. Fill the pan with the batter.
4. Bake for 25 to 30 minutes in the preheated oven, or until a knife inserted in the center comes out clean. Place in the refrigerator to completely cool.

5. To remove cake from pan, run a table knife around the edges of the cake. Carefully invert onto a serving plate. Select how you want to split, fill, and frost.

Roasted Garlic Lemon Broccoli

Ingredients

- 2 heads broccoli, separated into florets
- 2 tsp. extra-virgin olive oil
- 1 tsp. sea salt
- ½ tsp. ground black pepper
- 1 clove garlic, minced
- ½ tsp. lemon juice

Directions

1. Set the oven to 400 degrees Fahrenheit (200 degrees C).
2. In a big bowl, combine broccoli florets with extra virgin olive oil, sea salt, pepper, and garlic. On a baking sheet, spread the broccoli out in an even layer.
3. Bake for 15 to 20 minutes, or until the florets are soft enough to pierce the stems with a fork, in the preheated oven. Transfer to a serving platter after removal.
4. Before serving, liberally squeeze lemon juice over broccoli for a cool, tangy finish.

Quinoa and Black Beans

Ingredients

- 1 tsp. vegetable oil
- 1 onion, chopped
- 3 cloves garlic, chopped
- ¾ cups of quinoa
- 1 ½ cups of vegetable broth
- 1 tsp. ground cumin
- ¼ tsp. cayenne pepper
- salt and ground black pepper to taste
- 1 cups of frozen corn kernels
- 2 (15 Oz.) cans black beans, rinsed and drained
- ½ cups of chopped fresh cilantro

Directions

1. Oil is heated in a big saucepan at a medium heat. Cook and stir for about 10 minutes, until the onion and garlic are just starting to soften.
2. Combine the quinoa with the onion mixture; pour the vegetable broth over the top; season with cumin, cayenne, salt, and pepper. Bring to a boil; cover, lower heat, and simmer for 20 minutes or until quinoa is tender and broth has been absorbed.
3. Frozen corn has been added; simmer for another 5 minutes or until thoroughly heated. Add the cilantro and the black beans.

Zucchini and Potato Bake

Ingredients

- 4 medium potatoes, peeled and cut into large chunks
- 2 medium zucchini, quartered and cut into large pieces
- 1 medium red bell pepper, seeded and chopped
- ½ cups of dry bread crumbs
- ¼ cups of olive oil
- 1 clove garlic, sliced
- paprika to taste
- salt and ground black pepper to taste

Directions

1. Set the oven to 400 degrees Fahrenheit (200 degrees C).
2. In a medium baking pan, combine the potatoes, zucchini, red bell pepper, bread crumbs, olive oil, and garlic. Add paprika, salt, and pepper for seasoning.
3. Potatoes should bake for about an hour in a preheated oven, stirring occasionally, until they are tender and lightly browned.

Sheet Pan Roasted Vegetables

Ingredients

- 8 zucchini, peeled and chopped

- 1 eggplant, peeled and diced
- 8 carrots, diced
- 16 cherry tomatoes
- 2 red onions, sliced
- 1 red bell pepper, sliced
- 1 yellow bell pepper, sliced
- ½ cups of olive oil
- 1 tsp. dried rosemary
- 1 tsp. dried thyme
- 2 bay leaves, crushed
- 1 tsp. dried oregano
- 2 cloves garlic, minced
- 2 tbsp. fresh lemon juice
- 1 tsp. grated lemon zest
- salt and pepper to taste

Directions

1. Combine the oil, rosemary, thyme, bay leaves, oregano, garlic, lemon juice, lemon zest, salt, and pepper in a large bowl with the zucchini, eggplant, carrots, tomatoes, onions, and peppers. For at least two hours and ideally overnight, cover and chill the dish.
2. Set oven to 400 degrees Fahrenheit (200 degrees C).
3. Roast the vegetables on a sizable roasting pan, uncovered, for 20 minutes, or until the tomatoes have split and some of the vegetables' edges are beginning to crisp. After taking it out of the oven, stir it, then put it back in for another 20 minutes. Turning the vegetables every 20 minutes, reduce heat to 200

degrees F (95 degrees C), and cook for an additional 20 minutes or until they are tender.

Spanish Rice II

Ingredients

- 2 tbsp. vegetable oil
- 1 cups of uncooked white rice
- 1 onion, chopped
- ½ green bell pepper, chopped
- 2 cups of water
- 1 (10 Oz.) can diced tomatoes and green chiles
- 2 tsp. chili powder, or to taste
- 1 tsp. salt

Directions

1. In a large skillet set over medium heat, heat the oil. Rice, onion, and bell pepper should be sautéed until the rice is browned and the onions are soft.
2. Add tomatoes and water and stir. Salt and chili powder are used to season. Once the liquid has been absorbed and the rice has cooked for 30 minutes, cover the pot and simmer.

Green Bean Curry

Ingredients

- 1 tbsp. vegetable oil
- 1 onion, sliced
- 1 serrano peppers, thinly sliced
- 1 clove garlic, crushed
- 5 fresh curry leaves
- 1 tbsp. curry powder
- ½ tsp. fenugreek seeds
- ¼ tsp. ground turmeric
- salt to taste
- 1 lb fresh green beans, trimmed
- ½ cups of coconut milk
- 2 tbsp. lime juice

Directions

1. In a saucepan, heat the oil to a medium-high temperature. Garlic, onion, serrano pepper, curry leaves, and oil are all cooked together until the onions are golden brown. Cook for an additional 3 minutes after adding the curry powder, fenugreek seeds, turmeric, and salt. Stir the mixture before adding the green beans, coating them completely. Cook the beans until they are al dente by reducing the heat to medium-low. Add the coconut milk, then simmer for at least five more minutes. Just before serving, remove from heat and stir in lime juice.

BREAKFAST

Cheesy Amish Breakfast Casserole

Ingredients

- 1 lb sliced bacon, diced
- 1 medium sweet onion, chopped
- 9 large eggs, lightly beaten
- 4 cups of frozen shredded hash brown potatoes, thawed
- 2 cups of shredded Cheddar cheese
- 1 ½ cups of small curd cottage cheese
- 1 ¼ cups of shredded Swiss cheese

Directions

1. Set the oven to 350 degrees Fahrenheit (175 degrees C). A 9x13-inch baking pan should be greased.
2. Bacon and onion should be cooked and stirred in a sizable skillet over medium-high heat for about 10 minutes, or until the bacon is evenly browned. Drain.
3. Add the onion and bacon to a big bowl. Add the eggs, potatoes, Swiss, Cheddar, and cottage cheese. Put the prepared baking dish with the mixture inside.

4. Bake for 45 to 50 minutes in a preheated oven, or until the eggs are set and the cheese is melted. 10 minutes should pass before cutting and serving.

Chorizo Breakfast Bowls

Ingredients

Pico de Gallo:

- 4 Roma tomatoes, diced
- ½ cups of diced sweet onion
- ¼ cups of chopped fresh cilantro
- 1 jalapeno pepper, seeded and minced
- 1 lime, juiced
- 1 tsp. minced garlic
- ⅛ tsp. garlic salt
- 1 (15.5 Oz.) can black beans, rinsed and drained
- 3 tbsp. olive oil, divided
- 2 (10 Oz.) bags frozen sweet potatoes
- salt and ground black pepper to taste
- 1 (1 lb) ground chorizo sausage
- 4 eggs
- 4 avocados, peeled and sliced
- ¼ cups of crumbled Cotija cheese
- 1 tsp. Mexican-style hot sauce

Directions

1. In a bowl, combine the tomatoes, onion, cilantro, jalapeno, lime juice, garlic salt, and minced garlic. Stir to combine. Add black beans and 1/2 cups of of pico de gallo to a different bowl. Place both bowls in the refrigerator with covers on.
2. A large skillet with 2 tbsp. of olive oil on medium heat. Salt and pepper the sweet potatoes after adding them. Cook and stir for 15 to 20 minutes, or until browned and crispy.
3. In the meantime, cook the chorizo for about 10 minutes, stirring frequently, in a second skillet over medium heat.
4. Four bowls should be filled with the cooked chorizo, sweet potatoes, black bean mixture, and avocado. Add some Cojita cheese.
5. A nonstick skillet should be heated to medium. the final tbsp. of olive oil. Eggs should be cracked into the pan and cooked for about a minute, or until the edges are opaque. Turn down the heat and cover the skillet. Cook for 4 to 6 minutes, or until the whites are set and the yolks are the desired firmness.
6. Each bowl should have an egg on top of it. Serve with more hot sauce and pico de gallo.

Big Bob's Big Brunch Quesadillas

Ingredients

- ½ small onion, chopped
- ½ tomato, chopped
- 1 jalapeno pepper, seeded and minced

- 1 sprig fresh cilantro, chopped
- 6 eggs, beaten
- 4 (10 inch) flour tortillas
- 2 cups of shredded Cheddar cheese
- ¼ cups of sour cream, for topping
- ¼ cups of guacamole, for topping

Directions

1. On high heat, place the chopped onion, tomato, jalapeno, and cilantro in the skillet. Cook until the meat is tender.
2. Crack eggs into the pan once the vegetables have softened. Allow eggs to fully cook on one side before flipping and cooking the other.
3. When the eggs are done, warm the tortillas through in the same skillet. On a plate, place one tortilla, followed by the egg mixture and cheese. Add 1 tbsp. of guacamole and 1 tbsp. of sour cream to each serving.

Hawaiian-Style Quesadillas

Ingredients

- 10 flour tortillas
- 1 ½ lbs sliced ham
- 3 (8 Oz.) packages shredded mozzarella and Cheddar cheese blend
- 1 (8 Oz.) jar salsa

- 1 (15 Oz.) can pineapple chunks, drained
- 1 (8 Oz.) carton sour cream

Directions

1. Griddle is heated over medium-high heat. A tortilla should be lightly toasted for 1 to 2 minutes. To heat through, place 2 to 3 ham slices on the griddle's opposite side. Toasted tortilla is turned over, sprinkled with mozzarella and cheddar cheese mixture, hot ham is layered on top, desired amount of salsa is spread on top, desired amount of pineapple is sprinkled on top, and tortilla is folded in half.
2. After 2 to 4 minutes, flip the quesadilla over and continue cooking until the cheese has melted and the tortilla is the desired crispness. Slice using a pizza cutter into wedges. Add the remaining ingredients and repeat. Sour cream is recommended.

Zucchini Breakfast Quesadilla

Ingredients

- 1 tsp. vegetable oil
- 1 medium zucchini, cut into 1/2-inch pieces
- 2 medium scallions, thinly sliced
- ¼ tsp. ground black pepper
- ⅛ tsp. dried oregano
- ⅛ tsp. crushed red pepper flakes

- 2 large eggs
- 1 tbsp. water
- ¼ cups of shredded Cheddar cheese
- ½ tsp. salt
- 4 (6 inch) flour tortillas

Directions

1. A 10-inch skillet should be heated to medium-high. Add the oil, followed by the zucchini, scallions, oregano, black pepper, and pepper flakes. Cook vegetables for 3 to 4 minutes, or until they are tender. Cook for two more minutes on low heat with a cover.
2. Crack eggs into a bowl in the meantime. Water should be added, and whisked in thoroughly. Add the salt and Cheddar cheese.
3. Increase the heat to medium-high after adding the egg mixture to the skillet. Until eggs are soft-set, stir and scramble for 3 to 5 minutes. After transferring the egg mixture to a plate, clean the skillet with a paper towel.
4. Each tortilla's half should have 1/4 of the egg mixture spread on it. Half-fold tortillas.
5. Set the pristine skillet over a medium-high flame. Two tortillas at a time, add to the hot skillet, and cook for about a minute on each side, or until crisp.

Crispy Rolled Breakfast Burrito

Ingredients

- 4 slices bacon
- 1 large russet potato, peeled and cubed
- salt and freshly ground black pepper to taste
- 1 pinch cayenne pepper, or to taste
- ¼ cups of sliced onion
- ¼ cups of sliced bell pepper
- 1 cups of grated Cheddar cheese
- 4 large eggs, beaten
- 2 (10 inch) flour tortillas
- 1 tsp. hot sauce, or to taste
- 1 medium avocado, cubed
- 2 tbsp. sour cream
- 1 tbsp. fresh cilantro leaves, or to taste

Directions

1. In a cold, nonstick pan over medium-high heat, add the bacon. Cook for 10 minutes or until browned, crisp, and foamy. Turn off the heat, transfer the food to a plate lined with paper towels, and reserve.
2. Put medium heat on the pan of bacon fat and add the cubed potatoes. Add cayenne, black pepper, and salt for seasoning. Cook, occasionally tossing and turning, for 8 to 10 minutes, or until the potatoes are browned, crispy, and soft. Add the onions and peppers, and cook for 2 to 3 minutes, or until they start to soften. To drain extra bacon fat, place everything in a strainer over a bowl.

3. Put two cooked bacon strips back in the pan to assemble one breakfast burrito. Spread half of the potato mixture throughout the pan and increase heat to medium. Pour two beaten eggs on top after evenly distributing half of the Cheddar cheese.
4. To ensure that the egg is distributed evenly, tilt the pan. Overlay a tortilla on top, gently pressing it into the remaining ingredients. Just cook for one minute, or until the eggs are firm enough to flip. With caution but assurance, turn everything over so that the tortilla is now on the bottom. Cook for 2 to 3 minutes, or until the tortilla is as crispy and browned as you prefer.
5. Transfer to a plate after being taken off the heat. Serve with hot sauce, avocado, sour cream, and cilantro after rolling into a burrito. Cook the remaining burrito by repeating.

Jimmy Dean Breakfast Casserole

Ingredients

- cooking spray
- 1 (16 Oz.) package Regular Flavor Jimmy Dean Pork Sausage
- 10 large eggs, lightly beaten
- 3 cups of milk
- 2 tsp. dry mustard
- 1 tsp. salt
- 6 cups of cubed bread
- 2 cups of shredded sharp Cheddar cheese

- 1 medium tomato, seeded and chopped
- ½ cups of sliced mushrooms
- ½ cups of thin-sliced green onion
- ½ tsp. black pepper

Directions

1. Set the oven to 325 degrees Fahrenheit (165 degrees C). Spray cooking oil in a 9x13-inch baking dish.
2. In a large skillet, cook sausage over medium-high heat, stirring frequently, for 8 to 10 minutes, or until thoroughly cooked and no longer pink. Get rid of the heat.
3. In a big bowl, stir together the salt, dry mustard, eggs, and milk.
4. Place the prepared dish with half the bread evenly distributed inside. Add half of the cheese, half of the tomato, half of the mushroom, half of the green onion, and half of the black pepper to the dish. Add another layer after the first. Over the casserole, evenly pour the egg mixture.
5. Bake uncovered for 55 to 60 minutes, or until eggs are set. If the top starts to brown too quickly, cover it with foil.

Farmer's Casserole

Ingredients

- cooking spray
- 3 cups of frozen hash brown potatoes
- ¾ cups of shredded pepper Jack cheese

- 1 cups of cooked ham, diced
- ¼ cups of chopped green onions
- 4 large eggs, beaten
- 1 (12 fluid Oz.) can evaporated milk
- ¼ tsp. ground black pepper
- ⅛ tsp. salt

Directions

1. Set the oven to 350 degrees Fahrenheit (175 degrees C).
2. Apply cooking spray to a 2-quart casserole dish.
3. Put hash brown potatoes in the bottom of the dish as evenly as possible. Sprinkle with pepper jack cheese, ham, and green onions in that order.
4. In a medium bowl, combine the eggs, pepper, salt, and evaporated milk. Overlay the layers in the dish with the egg mixture.
5. Bake in the preheated oven for 40 to 45 minutes, or until a knife inserted in the center comes out clean.
6. Before serving, remove from the oven and let stand for five minutes.

Breakfast Migas

Ingredients

Tortilla Chips:

- ½ cups of oil for frying
- 12 (6 inch) corn tortillas, cut into bite-sized pieces
- salt to taste

Salsa:

- 3 dried guajillo chilies
- 5 medium Roma tomatoes
- 2 cloves garlic, peeled
- ¼ cups of chopped onion
- 3 cups of hot water
- 2 tsp. salt, divided
- ¼ tsp. dried Mexican oregano
- ⅛ tsp. ground cumin
- 1 pinch ground black pepper
- 1 tbsp. vegetable oil

Migas:

- 5 large eggs, beaten
- 3 medium green onions, chopped
- ¼ cups of fresh cilantro leaves
- 1 ripe avocado, pitted and sliced
- 2 tbsp. shredded Oaxaca cheese, or to taste

Directions

1. Add enough oil to the skillet to cover it by 1 inch and place it on the stovetop at medium heat. When the oil is hot, add the cut tortilla pieces sparingly to the skillet. Fry the tortilla pieces in the hot oil for two to three minutes, or until they are golden and crisp. With a slotted spoon, remove the tortilla chips and

place them on a plate with paper towels underneath to drain. As you work in batches to finish frying all of the tortilla pieces, season with salt to taste. Set aside the frying oil.

2. For about 20 seconds on each side, toast guajillo chiles in a flat griddle or comal over medium-low heat until fragrant.
3. In a saucepan, combine tomatoes, garlic, and toasted chiles. Pour hot water over the mixture. Approximately 10 minutes of simmering at medium-low heat is required to completely cook the tomatoes and soften the guajillos. Save half a cups of of cooking liquid.
4. Blend the reserved liquid with the tomatoes, garlic, onion, oregano, cumin, and 1 tsp. of salt. Blend until smooth on high. sift the sauce.
5. In a pan over medium-high heat, warm 1 tbsp. of vegetable oil. When the oil is hot, add the sauce and let it simmer for 12 to 15 minutes until the salsa is thick. If necessary, adjust the seasoning.
6. A skillet with one tbsp. of the saved frying oil is heated to medium-high heat. Once the oil is hot, add all of the tortilla chips, and reheat for one minute. Add the eggs, then cook and stir them until they start to set. For about two minutes, until the eggs are cooked and the salsa is evenly distributed throughout, add the salsa and gently fold it into the egg mixture.
7. Remove from the heat, then top with cheese, avocado, green onions, and cilantro.

Super Easy Breakfast Sausage Loaf

Ingredients

- 1 serving cooking spray
- 1 lb bulk pork sausage
- ¼ cups of brown sugar
- 1 tbsp. butter
- 4 large eggs
- 2 tbsp. milk
- 1 pinch salt and ground black pepper to taste
- 1 (8 Oz.) package refrigerated crescent rolls
- 1 cups of shredded Colby-Monterey Jack cheese

Directions

1. Set oven to 375 degrees Fahrenheit (190 degrees C). A 9x5-inch loaf pan should be sprayed with cooking oil.
2. Brown sugar and sausage are mixed together as a large skillet is heated over medium-high heat. Cook and stir the meat until it is browned all over, crumbly, and no longer pink. Extra grease should be drained and thrown away. After transferring the sausage to a bowl, clean the skillet.
3. In a clean skillet over low heat, melt the butter. Combine the eggs, milk, salt, and black pepper in a bowl. Fill the skillet with the eggs. Allow the eggs to cook without stirring until they start to set, then gently stir the eggs for 5 to 7 minutes, or until the curds are distinct and set but not dry.

4. Roll out the crescent roll dough, and use 3/4 of it to line the bottom and sides of the prepared pan. The remaining 1/4 of the dough should then be placed on top of the sausage, scrambled eggs, and Colby-Monterey Jack cheese layers in the pan. Pinch the dough's edges and corners together.
5. Bake for 25 to 30 minutes in a preheated oven, or until golden brown.

Breakfast Paella

Ingredients

- 1 tbsp. olive oil
- ½ cups of chopped onion
- ½ cups of chopped red bell pepper
- ½ cups of chopped Spanish chorizo
- 2 cloves garlic, minced
- 1 cups of medium-grain white rice
- ½ tsp. salt
- ½ tsp. smoked paprika
- 1 pinch saffron threads
- 2 cups of low-sodium chicken broth
- 1 (15 Oz.) can red kidney beans, rinsed and drained
- ½ cups of sofrito sauce
- ¼ cups of green olives, pitted and chopped
- 2 bay leaves
- 1 cups of frozen peas

- 4 large eggs
- chopped fresh parsley
- lemon wedges, for serving

Directions

1. Over medium heat, preheat the oil in a large cast iron skillet or paella pan. Add chorizo, onion, and bell pepper. Cook, frequently stirring, for about 5 minutes or until vegetables soften. Add the garlic and cook for 30 seconds or until fragrant. Add salt, paprika, saffron, and rice. Cook for about a minute, stirring frequently, until rice is just beginning to toast.
2. Beans, sofrito, olives, and bay leaves should all be added. up to a boil. Reduce heat, cover, and simmer for 12 to 15 minutes, or until rice is nearly done but still firm to the bite. Remove and throw away the bay leaves.
3. Peas should be gently folded in while being mindful not to scratch the skillet's bottom. Create 4 holes in the rice. Put an egg into each depression. Cook covered for 7 to 10 minutes, or until the whites are set and the yolks are thick. Serve with lemon wedges and parsley as garnish (if using).

Chaffles with Almond Flour

Ingredients

- 1 large egg
- 1 tbsp. blanched almond flour

- ¼ tsp. baking powder
- ½ cups of shredded mozzarella cheese
- cooking spray

Directions

1. In a bowl, combine the egg, baking powder, and almond flour. Add the mozzarella cheese, then set the batter aside.
2. As directed by the manufacturer, preheat a waffle iron.
3. Cooking spray should be applied to the waffle maker's both sides before use. Spread out the batter with a spoon starting in the center after ladling half of it onto the waffle iron. Close the waffle maker and cook the pancakes for about 3 minutes, or until they are the desired doneness. Lift the waffle carefully out of the waffle maker, then proceed with the remaining batter. Give the chaffles two to three minutes to cool and crisp up.

Christmas Breakfast Sausage Casserole

Ingredients

- 1 lb ground pork sausage
- 1 tsp. mustard powder
- ½ tsp. salt
- 4 eggs, beaten
- 2 cups of milk
- 6 slices white bread, toasted and cut into cubes
- 8 Oz. mild Cheddar cheese, shredded

Directions

1. Add sausage crumbles to a medium skillet. Cook until evenly browned over medium heat; drain.
2. Combine the mustard powder, salt, eggs, and milk in a medium bowl. Stir to evenly distribute the cheese, bread cubes, and sausage. Fill a 9x13-inch baking dish with oil. For eight hours or overnight, cover and chill the dish in the refrigerator.
3. Set oven to 350 degrees Fahrenheit (175 degrees C).
4. Bake for 45 to 60 minutes with a cover. Remove the cover and lower the temperature to 325 °F (165 degrees C). Bake for a further 30 minutes, or until the mixture is set.

DESSERTS

Chocolate Trifle

Ingredients

- 1 (18.25 Oz.) package brownie mix
- 1 large egg
- ¾ cups of water, divided
- ¼ cups of vegetable oil
- 1 (14 Oz.) can sweetened condensed milk

- 1 (3.9 Oz.) package instant chocolate pudding mix
- 1 (8 Oz.) container frozen whipped topping, thawed
- 1 (12 Oz.) container frozen whipped topping, thawed
- 1 (1.5 Oz.) bar chocolate candy

Directions

1. Set the oven to 350 degrees Fahrenheit (175 degrees C). A 9-inch square glass baking pan should be greased.
2. In a big bowl, mix the brownie mix, egg, 1/4 cups of water, and vegetable oil. Stir for about 50 strokes, or until thoroughly combined. Apply the mixture to the prepared pan.
3. Bake in the preheated oven for 25 to 30 minutes, or until a toothpick inserted 1 inch from the edges comes out clean. After taking the food out of the oven, give it 30 minutes to cool completely.
4. Cut the 1-inch squares of cooled brownies and set them aside.
5. In a big bowl, mix together condensed milk, remaining 1/2 cups of water, and pudding mix. Until there are no more streaks, fold in 8 Oz. of whipped topping.
6. Put half of the brownies in a glass serving dish or trifle bowl. Half of the 12-Oz. container of whipped topping is placed on top, followed by half of the pudding mixture. recur in layers. As a garnish, shave some chocolate on top.
7. 8 hours before serving, refrigerate.

Cookie Balls

Ingredients

- 1 lb chocolate sandwich cookies, crushed
- 1 (8 Oz.) package cream cheese, softened
- 1 lb vanilla-flavored candy coating, melted

Directions

In a large mixing bowl, combine crushed cookies and cream cheese to form a stiff dough. Roll into balls and dip with a fork in melted candy coating.

Let rest on waxed paper until set, about 30 minutes.

Tiger Butter Chocolates

Ingredients

1 lb white baking chocolate, coarsely chopped

1 cups of natural peanut butter

5 Oz. dark chocolate, coarsely chopped

Directions

1. A 9x13-inch baking dish should be lined with plastic wrap.
2. White chocolate should be melted in the top of a double boiler set over simmering water. To prevent scorching, stir the chocolate frequently and scrape the sides with a rubber spatula.

3. In a sizable bowl, combine the melted white chocolate with the peanut butter. Fill baking dish with the mixture, then use a spatula to smooth the top.
4. Dark chocolate should be melted in the top of a double boiler set over simmering water. To prevent scorching, stir the chocolate frequently and scrape the sides with a rubber spatula. Stripes of melted dark chocolate should be drizzled over the white chocolate-peanut butter mixture. Make a marble pattern with a butter knife.
5. Allow candy to set for 45 minutes or until it starts to firm up but is still liquid. Square them up.

Cocoa Powder Chocolate Mousse

Ingredients

- ½ cups of heavy whipping cream
- 2 tbsp. unsweetened cocoa powder
- 2 tbsp. powdered sugar
- ¼ tsp. vanilla extract
- 1 pinch salt

Directions

1. Using an electric mixer, combine heavy whipping cream, cocoa powder, powdered sugar, vanilla extract, and salt in a big bowl and beat until stiff peaks form.

2. In six shot glasses, pipe the mousse. Serve right away or wait to serve while chilled.

Ultimate Chocolate Dessert

Ingredients

- 4 Oz. bittersweet chocolate, chopped
- ½ tsp. instant coffee
- 1 pinch salt
- 1 cups of heavy cream
- 3 tbsp. white sugar
- ½ tsp. vanilla extract

Directions

1. In a medium bowl, mix the chocolate, instant coffee, and salt.
2. Cream, sugar, and vanilla are heated in a saucepan over medium heat while being constantly stirred until the mixture barely simmers.
3. Give the chocolate mixture a minute to absorb the hot cream mixture.
4. For one to two minutes, whisk the chocolate and cream mixture to combine.
5. Four tiny espresso cups of should be filled with the mixture. To get rid of any air bubbles, tap. Spend at least four hours in the refrigerator to thoroughly chill.

6. Serve with grated chocolate on top, or top with light whipped cream and cocoa powder.

Chocolate Banana Sorbet

Ingredients

- 4 ripe bananas, peeled and frozen
- ¼ cups of cocoa powder
- 3 tbsp. powdered sugar
- 1 tsp. vanilla extract
- 1 tsp. instant coffee granules

Directions

1. In a strong blender, such as a Vitamix, combine bananas, cocoa powder, powdered sugar, vanilla extract, and instant coffee. Blend all the ingredients together while using the tamper. Serve right away or, for a firmer texture, freeze for three hours in a freezer-safe container.

Éclair Cake

Ingredients

- 3 cups of milk

- 1 (8 Oz.) container frozen whipped topping, thawed
- 2 (3.5 Oz.) packages instant vanilla pudding mix
- 1 (16 Oz.) package graham cracker squares
- 1 (16 Oz.) package prepared chocolate frosting

Directions

1. In a medium bowl, thoroughly combine the pudding mix, milk, and whipped topping.
2. In a 9x13-inch baking pan, arrange graham cracker squares in a single layer. Spread the crackers evenly with half of the pudding mixture, followed by another layer of crackers and the remaining pudding mixture. Add one more layer of Graham crackers on top. 30 minutes of refrigeration under cover.
3. Frost the chilled cake, going all the way to the pan's edges. Before serving, re-cover and chill for at least 3 1/2 hours.

Crazy Cake

Ingredients

- 3 cups of all-purpose flour
- 2 cups of white sugar
- 1 tsp. salt
- 2 tsp. baking soda
- ½ cups of unsweetened cocoa powder
- ¾ cups of vegetable oil
- 2 tbsp. distilled white vinegar

- 2 tsp. vanilla extract
- 2 cups of cold water

Directions

1. Sift the following ingredients into a 9 x 13 inch ungreased cake pan: flour, sugar, salt, soda, and cocoa. Creating three wells Fill the first well with oil, the second with vinegar, and the third with vanilla. Add cold water to the mixture and thoroughly stir with a fork.
2. Bake for 30 to 40 minutes, or until a toothpick inserted comes out clean, at 350 degrees F (175 degrees C). Using your preferred icing, frost.

Dessert Crepes

Ingredients

- 4 eggs, lightly beaten
- 1 ⅓ cups of milk
- 1 cups of all-purpose flour
- 2 tbsp. butter, melted
- 2 tbsp. white sugar
- ½ tsp. salt

Directions

1. In a big bowl, stir the eggs, milk, flour, melted butter, sugar, and salt until everything is well combined.

2. Over medium heat, preheat a medium skillet or crepe pan. Use a paper towel or a small amount of oil or butter to lightly grease the pan.
3. About 3 tbsp. of crepe batter should be poured onto the hot pan using a serving spoon or small ladle. Tilt the pan to coat the bottom surface evenly. Serve warm after cooking for 1 to 2 minutes per side until golden brown.

Best Brownies

Ingredients

- ½ cups of butter
- 1 cups of white sugar
- 2 eggs
- 1 tsp. vanilla extract
- ⅓ cups of unsweetened cocoa powder
- ½ cups of all-purpose flour
- ¼ tsp. salt
- ¼ tsp. baking powder

Frosting:

- 3 tbsp. butter, softened
- 3 tbsp. unsweetened cocoa powder
- 1 tbsp. honey
- 1 tsp. vanilla extract
- 1 cups of confectioners' sugar

Directions

1. Set oven to 350 degrees Fahrenheit (175 degrees C). An 8-inch square pan should be greased and floured.
2. Melt half a cups of of butter in a big pot. Add sugar, eggs, and 1 tsp. vanilla after taking the pan off the heat. Mix in 1/2 cups of flour, salt, baking powder, and 1/3 cups of cocoa. To the prepared pan, spread the batter.
3. Bake for 25 to 30 minutes in a preheated oven. Avoid overcooking.
4. After brownies have finished baking, prepare frosting. Combine 1 cups of confectioners' sugar, 1 tsp. vanilla extract, 3 tbsp. honey, 3 tbsp. cocoa, and 3 tbsp. softened butter. until smooth, stir.
5. While brownies are still warm, frost them.

Toasted Waffle Ice Cream Sandwich

Ingredients

- 1 frozen waffle
- ½ tbsp. butter
- 1 scoop vanilla ice cream, softened
- 1 tbsp. maple syrup

Directions

1. After cutting the frozen waffle in half, immediately spread it with butter and toast it. On one half of the waffle, evenly distribute a scoop of ice cream. Place the other half of the waffle on top of the ice cream and gently press to seal the sandwich. Drizzle the ice cream with maple syrup.

Easy Strawberry Shortcake

Ingredients

- 1 quart fresh strawberries, sliced
- ¼ cups of white sugar
- 1 (12 Oz.) package prepared sponge cake dessert cups of
- 1 (7 Oz.) can whipped cream, or to taste

Directions

1. Strawberries should be placed in a bowl with sugar; stir to combine. Cover and chill for about 15 minutes, or until sugar dissolves.
2. In each serving bowl, put one dessert cups of and top with strawberries. Add some whipped cream to each.

Simple Strawberry Sauce

Ingredients

- 2 quarts fresh strawberries, cleaned, hulled and sliced
- ½ cups of white sugar

Directions

1. Strawberries should be put in a big bowl. Over the berries, evenly sprinkle the sugar; toss to combine. Allow to stand for 10 minutes at room temperature while stirring occasionally.
2. Until you're ready to serve, cover and chill the food in the fridge.

Strawberry Rhubarb Pie

Ingredients

- 2 ¼ cups of all-purpose flour
- 1 tsp. salt
- ½ cups of vegetable oil
- 6 tbsp. milk
- 5 medium stalks rhubarb, cut into 1 1/2 inch pieces
- 1 ½ cups of sliced fresh strawberries
- 1 ½ cups of white sugar
- 3 ½ tbsp. tapioca
- 1 pinch salt
- 1 ½ tsp. ground nutmeg

Directions

1. Salt and flour should be combined in a sizable bowl to make the crust. In a measuring cups of with a 1 cups of capacity, add the 6 tbsp. of milk on top of the 1/2 cups of oil. NEVER MIX! With a fork, combine milk and oil over the flour until a dough ball forms. Make two balls out of the dough. Put one ball on a waxed paper sheet. Roll out to fit your pie plate, then place another sheet of waxed paper on top. Repeat with the remaining dough ball. Flip one of the crusts into the pie plate after removing the top paper. Press dough into paper after removing it. Keep any leftover dough for the top crust.
2. Set oven to 425 degrees Fahrenheit (220 degrees C).
3. Making Filling To thoroughly coat the fruit, combine the rhubarb, strawberries, sugar, tapioca, salt, and nutmeg. After adding butter, pour the filling into the crust. Cut three 1 inch slits in the top crust, cover, and seal the edges.
4. Pie should be baked for 20 minutes at 425 degrees F (175 degrees C). Bake for an additional 20 minutes at 375 degrees F (190 degrees C) reduced temperature. Pie should cool before being cut.

SALADS

Curry Chicken Salad

Ingredients

- 3 cooked skinless, boneless chicken breast halves, chopped
- 3 stalks celery, chopped
- ½ cups of low-fat mayonnaise
- 2 tsp. curry powder

Directions

1. Combine the chicken, celery, mayonnaise, and curry powder in a medium bowl.

Fruited Curry Chicken Salad

Ingredients

- 4 skinless, boneless chicken breast halves - cooked and diced
- 1 stalk celery, chopped
- ½ onion, chopped
- 1 small apple - peeled, cored and chopped
- ⅓ cups of golden raisins
- ⅓ cups of seedless green grapes, halved
- ½ cups of chopped toasted pecans
- ⅛ tsp. ground black pepper
- ½ tsp. curry powder

- ¾ cups of mayonnaise

Directions

1. Combine the chicken, celery, onion, apple, raisins, grapes, pecans, pepper, curry powder, and mayonnaise in a sizable salad bowl. Combine everything and coat by tossing. It's time to serve the salad!

Waldorf Goat Cheese Salad

Ingredients

- 2 cups of red leaf lettuce - rinsed, dried and torn
- 2 tbsp. raspberry walnut vinaigrette
- ½ cups of seedless red grapes, halved
- 2 tbsp. crumbled goat cheese
- 2 tbsp. chopped pecans

Directions

1. In a mixing bowl, combine the dressing with the lettuce; transfer to a serving dish. Enjoy with a topping of grapes, goat cheese, and pecans.

Morgan's Waldorf Salad

Ingredients

- 1 Granny Smith apple, cubed
- 1 Golden Delicious apple, cubed
- 1 Gala apple, cubed
- 1 Bosc pear, cubed
- 3 ribs celery, chopped
- ¾ cups of sweetened dried cranberries
- ½ cups of chopped walnuts
- ¼ cups of chopped pecans
- 1 cups of sour cream
- ¾ cups of mayonnaise
- 1 tbsp. granulated cane sugar
- 2 tsp. fresh lemon juice

Directions

1. In a sizable bowl, mix celery, cranberries, walnuts, pecans, Gala, Bosc, Golden Delicious, and Granny Smith apples.
2. For the dressing, combine sour cream, mayonnaise, sugar, and lemon juice in a different bowl.
3. Add dressing to apple mixture and stir to coat evenly. Before serving, let food cool in the refrigerator for at least 15 minutes.

Grilled Chicken Taco Salad

Ingredients

- 1 (15 Oz.) can black beans, rinsed and drained
- ¾ cups of medium-hot salsa
- ½ cups of chopped fresh cilantro
- 1 tbsp. lime juice
- 2 tbsp. chili powder
- 1 tsp. ground cumin
- 1 tsp. ground coriander
- 1 tsp. brown sugar
- ¼ tsp. cayenne pepper
- 1 tbsp. olive oil
- 1 lb skinless, boneless chicken breast halves
- 4 (7 inch) corn tortillas
- 4 cups of shredded lettuce
- ½ cups of chopped fresh cilantro
- 1 avocado - peeled, pitted, and sliced
- 1 lime, cut into wedges
- ¼ cups of sour cream

Directions

1. Set an outdoor grill to medium-high heat and give the grates a quick oiling.
2. In a bowl, combine the black beans, salsa, half the cilantro, and the lime juice.
3. Rub mixture over chicken breasts by combining chili powder, cumin, coriander, brown sugar, cayenne pepper, and olive oil in a bowl.
4. Cook chicken breasts on a heated grill for 10 to 12 minutes per side or until the juices run clear and the center is no longer pink. In the center, an instant-read thermometer should

register at least 165 degrees Fahrenheit (74 degrees C). Place the tortillas on the grill and cook them for 3 to 5 minutes, or until they are just beginning to lightly brown on both sides.

5. Slice the chicken into long, thin strips after transferring it to a cutting board. On top of the tortillas, distribute the chicken strips, the bean mixture, the lettuce, and the final 1/2 cups of of cilantro. Serve with sour cream, avocado, and lime wedges.

Easy Black Bean Taco Salad

Ingredients

- 1 lb ground beef
- 1 envelope taco seasoning mix
- ¾ cups of water
- 1 (15 Oz.) can black beans, drained
- 1 head romaine lettuce, shredded
- 1 (8 Oz.) jar salsa
- 2 tomatoes, diced
- 2 cups of shredded Mexican cheese blend
- 8 Oz. sour cream
- 1 (10 Oz.) bag tortilla chips

Directions

1. Over medium heat, cook ground beef in a skillet until crumbly and no longer pink, about 8 minutes; then, stir in taco

seasoning and water. About 10 more minutes of cooking will thicken the beef mixture.
2. Black beans should be added to a pan and heated to a simmer.
3. To make four salads, spread 1/4 of the beef mixture and 1/4 of the black beans on a serving plate. Repeat with the remaining beef mixture and beans. Salads should have distinct layers of romaine lettuce, salsa, tomatoes, and cheese. Add tortilla chips and sour cream liberally as garnish.

Jen's Heavenly Egg Salad

Ingredients

- 6 eggs
- ¼ cups of mayonnaise
- 1 tsp. Dijon mustard
- ½ tsp. prepared yellow mustard
- ½ lemon, juiced
- ¼ cups of chopped green onions
- salt and pepper to taste

Directions

1. Put an egg in a pan and pour cold water over it. Once the water has reached a rolling boil, turn off the heat. For 10 to 12 minutes, cover the eggs and let them sit in hot water. After removing from the hot water, peel. Place the eggs in an ice bath before peeling for a quicker cooling process.

2. Mayonnaise, Dijon mustard, yellow mustard, lemon juice, and green onions should all be combined in a medium bowl. Largely chop the eggs, then gently fold in the dressing. Add salt and pepper to taste.

Georgia Cracker Salad

Ingredients

- 1 (4 Oz.) packet saltine crackers
- 1 large tomato, chopped
- 3 green onions, finely chopped
- 1 ½ cups of mayonnaise
- 1 hard-cooked egg, chopped
- salt and freshly ground black pepper to taste

Directions

1. Add the saltines to a medium bowl and coarsely crumble them. Add the mayonnaise, tomato, and onions. Salt and pepper to taste, then stir in the hard-boiled egg.

Top Ramen Salad

Ingredients

Salad:

- 2 (3 Oz.) packages chicken-flavored ramen noodles, broken into pieces, seasoning packets reserved
- ½ cups of raw sunflower seeds
- ½ cups of slivered almonds
- 1 (16 Oz.) package coleslaw mix
- 3 green onions, chopped

Dressing:

- ½ cups of olive oil
- 3 tbsp. white vinegar
- 1 tbsp. white sugar
- ½ tsp. ground black pepper

Directions

2. Set the oven to 350 degrees Fahrenheit (175 degrees C). On a baking sheet, distribute almonds, sunflower seeds, and ramen noodles.
3. Bake the noodle mixture in the preheated oven for 10 to 15 minutes, or until fragrant and toasted. After cooling to room temperature, set aside.
4. In a sizable bowl, combine the coleslaw mix and green onions; top with the cooled noodle mixture.
5. Produce dressing: In a bowl, combine the olive oil, vinegar, sugar, black pepper, and any saved ramen seasoning packets. Whisk to combine well.
6. Toss the noodle mixture with the dressing to coat.

Smashed Cucumber Salad

Ingredients

- 2 English cucumbers
- 1 ½ tsp. kosher salt, plus more as needed
- 1 tsp. white sugar
- 2 cloves garlic, finely crushed
- 2 tbsp. seasoned rice vinegar
- 1 tsp. soy sauce
- 1 tsp. sesame oil
- red pepper flakes to taste
- 2 tsp. toasted sesame seeds

Directions

1. In order to reduce splattering, wrap each cucumber in plastic wrap. When the cucumbers start to crack and become slightly flattened, place them on a work surface and lb them with a flat object (like a meat lb). Take out of plastic. Cut cucumbers in half, lengthwise, and then in half again. Slices should be between 1 and 1 1/2 inches wide. Transfer to a bowl-over-a-strainer arrangement.
2. Sprinkle salt and sugar over the cucumber and combine thoroughly. For the cucumber pieces to drain into the bowl, place the strainer and bowl in the refrigerator for 30 to 60 minutes.
3. In a sizable bowl, combine the garlic, seasoned rice vinegar, soy sauce, sesame oil, and red pepper flakes. Whisk well.

4. Place the drained cucumbers in the dressing-filled bowl. Coat by tossing. Refrigerate for about 30 minutes to allow flavors to meld. Cover with plastic wrap.
5. Sesame seeds should be added to a serving bowl of cucumbers.

Tomato Mozzarella Salad

Ingredients

- 3 large tomatoes, sliced
- 8 Oz. mozzarella cheese, sliced
- ¼ cups of olive oil
- ¼ cups of balsamic vinegar
- ¼ tsp. salt
- ⅛ tsp. ground black pepper
- ¼ cups of minced fresh basil

Directions

1. On a sizable serving platter, arrange mozzarella and tomato slices alternately.
2. In a jar with a tight-fitting lid, combine the oil, balsamic vinegar, salt, and pepper; shake well. Sprinkle basil on top of the tomatoes, mozzarella, and drizzle.

Puffed Caramel Corn

Ingredients

- 1 (8 Oz.) bag corn puffs
- 1 cups of salted peanuts
- 1 cups of butter
- 1 cups of packed brown sugar
- ½ cups of light corn syrup
- 1 tsp. baking soda

Directions

1. Set the oven to 250 degrees Fahrenheit (120 degrees C).
2. In a sizable roasting pan, mix the corn puffs and peanuts.
3. In a large 2-quart saucepan, bring the butter, brown sugar, and corn syrup to a boil. For two minutes, cook and stir. Take the mixture off the heat and stir in the baking soda until it foams. Utilizing rubber spatulas, pour over corn puff mixture and thoroughly combine.
4. For about 45 minutes, or until a cooled piece of corn is crunchy, bake in the preheated oven, stirring every 10 to 15 minutes.
5. To cool, spread on wax paper. Divide into pieces and keep in an airtight container.

Pigs in a Blanket

Ingredients

- 1 (10 Oz.) package refrigerated biscuit dough
- 8 slices American processed cheese
- 8 frankfurters

Directions

1. Set the oven to 350 degrees Fahrenheit (175 degrees C).
2. Using a portion of biscuit dough, create a circle with a 3-inch diameter. A frankfurter is placed in the middle of the dough slice, which is then rolled up. Place the seam-side down on a cookie sheet. Repeat with the remaining dough sections.
3. Bake the biscuits in the preheated oven for 10 to 15 minutes, or until golden brown. Serve warm.

Buffalo Chicken Dip

Ingredients

- 2 (10 Oz.) cans chunk chicken, drained
- ¾ cups of hot pepper sauce
- 2 (8 Oz.) packages cream cheese, softened

- 1 cups of ranch dressing
- 1 ½ cups of shredded Cheddar cheese
- 1 bunch celery, cut into 4-inch pieces
- 1 (8 Oz.) box chicken-flavored crackers

Directions

1. Cook the chicken and hot pepper sauce in a skillet over medium heat for 3 to 5 minutes, or until thoroughly heated. Ranch dressing and cream cheese are combined. Cook and stir for 3 to 5 minutes, or until thoroughly combined and warm.
2. Add half of the Cheddar cheese after combining, then pour the mixture into a slow cooker. The remaining cheese should be added on top.
3. For 35 minutes or so, cook the dip on Low with the cover on.
4. Serve with crackers and celery sticks.

Southern Pimento Cheese

Ingredients

- 2 cups of shredded extra-sharp Cheddar cheese
- 8 Oz. cream cheese, softened
- ½ cups of mayonnaise
- ¼ tsp. garlic powder
- ¼ tsp. ground cayenne pepper
- ¼ tsp. onion powder
- 1 jalapeno pepper, seeded and minced

- 1 (4 Oz.) jar diced pimento, drained
- salt and black pepper to taste

Directions

1. In the large bowl of a mixer, combine the Cheddar cheese, cream cheese, mayonnaise, garlic powder, cayenne pepper, onion powder, minced jalapeno, and pimento. Beat at a medium speed, preferably with a paddle, until completely combined. Add salt and black pepper to taste.

Chocolate Peanut Butter Cups of

Ingredients

- 1 (11.5 Oz.) package milk chocolate chips, divided
- 1 cups of peanut butter
- ¼ tsp. salt
- ½ cups of confectioners' sugar

Directions

1. 12 paper muffin cups of liners should have their height cut in half.
2. In a container that can go in the microwave, put 1/2 chocolate chips. Stirring after each minute of the two minutes in the microwave. Half-fill each muffin cups of with melted chocolate. Draw the chocolate up the sides of the cups of with a spoon until it is completely covered. Refrigerate until completely firm.

3. Combine peanut butter, confectioners' sugar, and salt in a small bowl. Divide among the cups of of chocolate. Spread the peanut butter on top of the melted remaining chocolate. Cups of edges should be covered in chocolate.

Halloween Fruit Snacks

Ingredients

- 4 Oz. dried apricots
- 4 Oz. dried peaches
- ½ lb seedless green grapes, halved
- 2 tbsp. confectioners' sugar
- 1 tsp. water, or as needed
- ¼ cups of small candy eyeballs

Directions

1. Place peaches and apricots on a platter. Using a toothpick, skewer a few grapes vertically and the final one horizontally (for the head).
2. Confectioners' sugar and water are combined to create a thin, a little bit sticky icing. Two candy eyes are adhered to each piece of fruit and the horizontal "head" of the grape caterpillar using icing.

Fabulous Football Dip

Ingredients

- 1 lb sausage
- 1 (10 Oz.) can diced tomatoes with green chile peppers
- 2 (8 Oz.) packages cream cheese, softened

Directions

1. Sausage should be cooked through and browned in a big skillet over medium heat.
2. Add cream cheese and tomatoes to the skillet. Cook the mixture, stirring occasionally, until the cheese has melted.

Amazing and Easy Chicken Wings

Ingredients

- 2 cups of brown sugar
- 1 cups of yellow mustard
- ¼ cups of soy sauce
- 5 lbs chicken wings, cut into thirds and tips discarded

Directions

1. In a bowl, combine brown sugar, mustard, and soy sauce. Put 1/4 cups of of the marinade for basting in a small bowl, cover it, and chill.
2. Put wings in a sizable bag that can be sealed. Continue coating the wings with the remaining marinade. For at least two hours and up to overnight, seal and marinate wings.
3. Set oven to 375 degrees Fahrenheit (190 degrees C).
4. Transfer chicken wings to a baking sheet after removing them from the resealable bag. Eliminate marinade.
5. Bake for 30 minutes in the preheated oven. Cook, basting every 10 minutes, until the chicken is no longer pink in the center, about 30 more minutes. Baste the wings with the reserved 1/4 cups of marinade.

Sheet Pan Nachos

Ingredients

- 1 lb ground beef (80% lean)
- ¼ cups of water
- 1 tbsp. chili powder
- 1 tsp. ground cayenne pepper
- salt and ground black pepper to taste
- 1 (14.5 Oz.) package tortilla chips
- 1 (4 Oz.) can sliced black olives
- 1 (12 Oz.) jar pickled jalapeno pepper slices
- 2 cups of shredded Cheddar cheese

- 1 (8 Oz.) container sour cream
- 1 cups of salsa

Directions

1. Set the oven's broiler to high and place a rack about 6 inches from the heat source. Aluminium foil is used to line a sheet pan.
2. A large skillet should be heated to medium-high. Cook and stir the beef in the hot skillet for 5 to 7 minutes, or until it is browned and crumbly. Combine with water, salt, pepper, cayenne, and chili powder.
3. Place tortilla chips on the baking sheet. Add the ground beef mixture on top. Add cheese, olives, and jalapeno slices on top.
4. For 3 to 5 minutes, broil cheese until bubbling and golden brown. Serve with salsa and sour cream for dipping.

Baked Jalapeño Poppers

Ingredients

- cooking spray
- 12 jalapeno peppers, halved lengthwise and seeded
- 2 Oz. cream cheese, softened
- 2 Oz. shredded Cheddar cheese
- ¼ cups of panko bread crumbs

Directions

1. Set the oven to 400 degrees Fahrenheit (200 degrees C). Apply cooking spray to a baking sheet.
2. Each jalapeo pepper half is filled with cream cheese, cheddar cheese, and bread crumbs, in that order, and then placed on the baking sheet that has been prepared.
3. About 20 minutes should pass in the preheated oven for the cheese to melt and the jalapenos to become tender.

SOUPS

Instant Pot Lasagna Soup

Ingredients

- 1 (4 Oz.) mild Italian sausage link, casing removed
- 1 lb ground sirloin
- 1 tbsp. olive oil
- 1 cups of finely chopped onion
- 1 tbsp. garlic, minced
- 1 (32 Oz.) can low-sodium chicken broth
- 24 Oz. marinara sauce
- 8 lasagna noodles, broken into pieces
- ½ tsp. salt
- ½ tsp. freshly ground black pepper

- 6 tsp. grated Parmesan cheese

Directions

1. Select the Sauté function on a multipurpose pressure cooker (such as an Instant Pot). Add the ground beef and sausage to the pot, cooking for about 5 minutes or until browned. Set aside the meat and drain and discard the grease. To ensure that the bottom of the pot is evenly coated, add the olive oil and stir. Add the onion and cook for about 5 minutes, until just soft but not browned. Add the garlic and cook for about a minute, until it is barely fragrant.
2. Deglazing the pan by adding chicken broth and scraping up the browned bits from the bottom. dispense the marinara sauce. Salt and pepper the meat mixture after adding them. To combine, stir. Make sure the lasagna noodles are completely covered in sauce before adding them. Lock the lid by closing it. Set the timer for 3 minutes while choosing high pressure in accordance with the manufacturer's instructions. Give the pressure 10 to 15 minutes to build.
3. Following the manufacturer's instructions, slowly release the pressure using the quick-release technique, which should take around 5 minutes. Lock released, lid removed. If necessary, taste and adjust the salt. Pour into bowls and sprinkle 1 tsp. of Parmesan cheese on top of each.

Geneva's Ultimate Hungarian Mushroom Soup

Ingredients

- 2 tbsp. unsalted butter
- 2 cups of chopped onions
- 1 ½ lbs fresh mushrooms, thickly sliced
- 4 ½ tsp. chopped fresh dill
- 1 tbsp. Hungarian sweet paprika
- 1 tbsp. soy sauce
- 2 cups of low-sodium chicken broth
- 1 cups of skim milk
- 3 tbsp. all-purpose flour
- ½ ripe tomato
- ½ Hungarian wax pepper
- 1 tsp. salt
- ground black pepper to taste
- ½ cups of light sour cream

Directions

1. In a sizable pot set over medium heat, melt the butter. In the butter, cook and stir the onions for about 5 minutes, or until fragrant. After adding the mushrooms, cook them for an additional 5 minutes or so, or until they are tender. The mushroom mixture has been combined with dill, paprika, soy sauce, and chicken broth. Heat has been turned down to low; cover and simmer for 15 minutes.

2. In a small bowl, combine the milk and flour. Add the mixture to the soup and stir. Tomato and Hungarian wax pepper should be added. Put the lid back on the pot and simmer for an additional 15 minutes while stirring occasionally. Add salt and pepper to taste. Stir in the sour cream, then cook and stir the soup for an additional 5 to 10 minutes, or until it has thickened. Before serving the soup, take out the tomato and Hungarian wax pepper and discard them.

Classic Vichyssoise

Ingredients

- 1 tbsp. butter
- 3 leeks, bulb only, sliced into rings
- 1 onion, sliced
- 5 medium potatoes, peeled and thinly sliced
- salt and pepper to taste
- ½ tsp. dried marjoram
- ¼ tsp. dried thyme
- 1 bay leaf
- 5 cups of chicken broth
- ¼ cups of heavy whipping cream

Directions

1. In a sizable stockpot set over low heat, melt the butter. Cover the pan and cook the leeks and onion for 10 minutes.

2. Potatoes are added after salt and pepper are added. Stir well after adding marjoram, thyme, and bay leaf. Cook for 12 minutes with a cover on.
3. dispense the chicken broth. Cook for 30 minutes with a lid partially on after bringing to a boil.
4. In a blender or food processor, puree the soup. After letting it reach room temperature, stir in the cream.

Cheeseburger Soup

Ingredients

- 4 tbsp. butter, divided
- ½ lb ground beef
- ¾ cups of chopped onion
- ¾ cups of shredded carrots
- ¾ cups of chopped celery
- 1 tsp. dried basil
- 1 tsp. dried parsley
- 4 cups of cubed potatoes
- 3 cups of chicken broth
- ¼ cups of all-purpose flour
- 1 ½ cups of milk
- 2 cups of cubed Cheddar cheese
- ¼ cups of sour cream

Directions

1. Melt the butter in a sizable stockpot over low heat. Leeks and onion should be cooked for 10 minutes in a covered pan.
2. After adding salt and pepper, potatoes are added. Add the bay leaf, marjoram, and thyme and stir well. With a cover on, cook for 12 minutes.
3. Give out the chicken stock. After bringing to a boil, cook for 30 minutes with a partially closed lid.
4. Puree the soup in a blender or food processor. Add the cream after it has reached room temperature.

French Spring Soup

Ingredients

- ¼ cups of butter
- 1 lb leeks, chopped
- 1 onion, chopped
- 2 quarts water
- 3 large potatoes, chopped
- 2 large carrots, chopped
- 1 bunch fresh asparagus, trimmed and cut into 1 inch pieces
- ⅓ cups of uncooked long-grain white rice
- 4 tsp. salt
- ½ lb fresh spinach
- 1 cups of heavy cream

Directions

1. In a sizable pot set over medium heat, melt the butter. Leeks and onion are added, and they are cooked until tender.
2. Fill up the pot with water. Add the rice, potatoes, carrots, and asparagus. Use salt to season. When the vegetables and rice are ready, bring to a boil, lower the heat, and simmer for 30 minutes.
3. Before serving, cook the soup mixture for another 5 minutes after adding heavy cream and spinach.

Best Cream Of Broccoli Soup

Ingredients

- 5 tbsp. butter, divided
- 1 onion, chopped
- 1 stalk celery, chopped
- 3 cups of chicken broth
- 8 cups of broccoli florets
- 3 tbsp. all-purpose flour
- 2 cups of milk
- ground black pepper to taste

Directions

1. In a small stockpot set over medium heat, melt 2 tbsp. of butter. Cook the onion and celery until they are soft. Cover and simmer the broccoli and broth for 10 minutes.

2. Fill the pitcher of the blender no more than halfway with the soup as you pour it in. When starting the blender, be sure to hold down the lid with a folded kitchen towel. Use a few quick pulses to get the soup moving in the blender before turning it on to puree. Pour into a clean pot after batch-pureeing until smooth. Alternately, you could puree the soup in the cooking pot using an immersion blender.
3. In a small saucepan over medium-low heat, melt 3 tbsp. of butter. Stir in the flour and milk. Add to soup and stir until thick and bubbly. Serve after adding pepper.

Cream of Fresh Asparagus Soup

Ingredients

- 1 lb fresh asparagus, trimmed and cut into 1 inch pieces
- 1 (14.5 Oz.) can chicken broth, divided
- ½ cups of chopped onion
- 2 tbsp. butter
- 2 tbsp. all-purpose flour
- 1 tsp. salt
- 1 pinch ground black pepper
- 1 cups of milk
- ½ cups of sour cream
- 1 tsp. fresh lemon juice

Directions

1. In a sizable pot, combine onion, 1/2 cups of chicken broth, and asparagus. Over high heat, cover and bring to a boil. Reduce heat to medium-low, cover, and simmer for 12 minutes or until asparagus is tender. Blend the mixture in a blender until it is completely smooth, then set it aside.
2. Melt butter over medium-low heat in the same pan. Add the flour, salt, and pepper, and continue to stir continuously for 2 minutes. As the mixture begins to boil, turn the heat up to medium; add the remaining chicken broth while stirring constantly. Add the milk and the pureed asparagus.
3. Pour a ladle of the hot soup into a small bowl with the sour cream, and then stir in the lemon juice. Without boiling, thoroughly reheat soup to serving temperature. Serve right away.

Stracciatella Soup

Ingredients

- 6 cups of chicken broth
- salt and freshly ground black pepper to taste
- 2 tbsp. semolina flour
- 3 large eggs
- 2 tbsp. chopped fresh parsley
- ½ Oz. grated Parmigiano-Reggiano cheese
- ½ Oz. grated pecorino Romano cheese
- 1 pinch cayenne pepper

- 1 pinch freshly grated nutmeg
- 1 tbsp. olive oil
- 1 pinch red pepper flakes

Directions

1. Over high heat, simmer the broth in the pot. When adjusting salt and pepper, taste the broth.
2. The following ingredients should be thoroughly combined in a bowl: eggs, parsley, semolina flour, grated Parmigiano Reggiano and pecorino Romano cheeses, salt, pepper, cayenne pepper, and nutmeg.
3. Slowly pour the egg mixture into the simmering broth while stirring. Reheat the mixture to a simmer. As the broth heats, the liquid will initially be slightly cloudy before becoming clear.
4. Serve in bowls and top with a few red pepper flakes and a drizzle of olive oil.

Chef John's Roasted Butternut Squash Soup

Ingredients

Soup:

- 1 tbsp. olive oil
- 1 chopped onion
- 1 cups of sliced carrots

- 6 whole garlic cloves, peeled
- 2 tsp. kosher salt, or to taste - divided
- 1 (3 1/2) lb butternut squash, halved lengthwise and seeded

Sage Brown Butter:

- 3 tbsp. unsalted butter
- 6 large sage leaves
- 6 cups of chicken broth, plus more if needed
- 2 tbsp. maple syrup
- 2 tbsp. cider vinegar
- 1 pinch cayenne pepper
- ½ cups of creme fraiche
- 1 tbsp. chopped fresh chives

Directions

1. Set oven to 400 degrees Fahrenheit (200 degrees C).
2. Olive oil should be added to a big roasting pan. Include the onion, carrots, garlic, and a dash of salt. until everything is well-oiled. Squash halves should be placed on the chopped vegetables flesh side up. Additional salt should be added to the squash.
3. Roast squash in a preheated oven for about an hour, or until it is soft and easily pierced with the tip of a knife. Give the vegetables some time to cool.
4. Melt butter in a medium-sized pan. Butter will begin to foam and turn a golden brown color. Low-heat setting. Remove pan from heat as soon as butter turns from golden to a pale, nutty brown, then stir in sage leaves. Stir to incorporate sage into the butter.

5. Scoop out the flesh of the squash and add it to the roasting pan with the chopped roasted vegetables. Place the mixture in a big stock pot. Add maple syrup, brown sage butter, and chicken broth by stirring. Set a pot over a high heat source and simmer. Reduce heat to low and simmer for 45 to 60 minutes to blend flavors. Get rid of the heat.
6. Utilizing an immersion blender, blend for 3 to 4 minutes, until very smooth. Mixture should be strained to get rid of any last bits of fibrous material.
7. Add a few tbsp. of water or chicken broth to the soup if it seems too thick. Add cayenne pepper, a dash of salt, and apple cider vinegar after stirring. Serves of soup should be topped with a dollop of creme fraiche and chives.

Chef John's Ham and Potato Soup

Ingredients

- 1 ½ lbs Yukon Gold potatoes, peeled and diced
- 1 medium onion, diced
- 1 medium carrot, diced
- 1 rib celery, diced
- 8 Oz. smoked ham, diced
- 3 cloves garlic, sliced
- 3 tbsp. butter
- ¼ cups of flour
- 4 cups of chicken broth

- 2 cups of water
- ½ cups of heavy cream
- salt and pepper to taste
- 1 pinch cayenne pepper
- 1 tbsp. chopped fresh chives for garnish

Directions

1. In a stockpot, melt the butter over medium heat until it turns golden. Cook and stir for 5 to 6 minutes, or until the ham is heated through. Add the carrot, celery, onion, and garlic.
2. Add flour and cook for about three minutes. 1 cups of of the chicken broth at a time, stir in. Stir in the water after adding it. Increase the temperature and bring to a simmer. 15 minutes of medium-low simmering with sporadically stirred.
3. If the soup needs more salt, taste it first and add it. Potatoes should be tender after 15 minutes of cooking after being stirred in. Delete fat if you like.
4. Mash the soup a few times with a potato masher, leaving lots of whole chunks of potato. Add cream, cayenne pepper, and salt and pepper to taste for seasoning. Heat through while stirring to combine. Fresh chives are a nice garnish.

Chef John's Minestrone Soup

Ingredients

- 2 tbsp. olive oil

- 3 Oz. chopped pancetta
- 1 onion, diced
- 1 cups of diced celery
- 4 cloves garlic, minced
- 4 cups of chicken broth
- 2 cups of water, plus more as needed
- 1 (28 Oz.) can plum tomatoes, crushed fine
- 1 cups of cranberry beans, shelled
- 2 cups of chopped cabbage, or more to taste
- 1 (15 Oz.) can garbanzo beans, drained
- 1 tsp. red pepper flakes, or to taste
- 1 tsp. Italian seasoning
- 2 tsp. salt
- 1 bunch Swiss chard, chopped
- ⅔ cups of ditalini pasta
- salt and ground black pepper
- ¼ cups of extra virgin olive oil, for drizzling
- ¼ cups of finely grated Parmigiano-Reggiano cheese
- ¼ cups of chopped fresh Italian flat-leaf parsley

Directions

1. In a large stock pot, warm 2 tbsp. of olive oil over medium-high heat. Add the pancetta, and cook and stir for 2 to 3 minutes, or until it starts to brown. Add celery and onions, and stir-fry for 3 minutes, or until onions begin to turn translucent. Once the garlic has been added, cook for another minute.
2. Add plum tomatoes, water, and chicken broth to the pancetta and onion mixture. Simmer for a while.

3. Combine the broth mixture with the cranberry beans, cabbage, garbanzo beans, red pepper flakes, Italian seasoning, and 2 tsp. of salt. Cook for 45 minutes, adding more water as necessary if the soup gets too thick, until the cranberry beans are tender.
4. Swiss chard is added and simmered for 15 minutes or until soft. To taste, add salt and black pepper to the food.
5. Add the pasta, raise the heat to medium-high, and simmer for about 15 minutes, or until the pasta is tender. Pour into bowls and garnish with Italian parsley, Parmigiano-Reggiano cheese, and extra virgin olive oil.

Printed in Great Britain
by Amazon

29399564R00071

LANDSCAPE, MONUMENTS AND SOCIETY